Pocket Guide

Choosing Woody Ornamentals

A concise
of woody landscape plants.

by
GERD KRÜSSMANN
Dendrologist

revised and translated by
Michael E. Epp
Horticulturist

TIMBER PRESS

in cooperation with
THE AMERICAN HORTICULTURAL SOCIETY

German edition published as
Krüssmann, *Taschenbuch der Gehölzverwendung*
© 1970 by Verlag Paul Parey
Berlin and Hamburg

English translation © 1982 by Timber Press, Inc.
All rights reserved.
Reprinted 1990, 1992

PRINTED IN SINGAPORE

TIMBER PRESS, INC.
9999 S.W. Wilshire, Suite 124
Portland, Oregon 97225

Library of Congress Cataloging in Publication Data

Krüssmann, Gerd.
  Pocket guide to chosing woody ornamentals.

  Translation of: Taschenbuch der Gehölzverwendung.
  1. Ornamental woody plants — Handbooks, manuals, etc.
I. Epp, Michael E.   II. Title
SB435.K77313   1982   635.9'77   82-13690
ISBN 0-917304-24-1

FOREWORD

"The underlying idea of the first edition of this book has remained the same: a working reference for garden designers, landscape contractors, home gardeners and above all, young gardeners."

Dortmund-Brunninghausen
(Botanic Garden)
West Germany

Summer 1970

Gerd Krüssmann

So, Herr Krüssmann summed up the intent of this book. It is indeed a working reference of which I have made great use, first as an apprentice gardener at the Dortmund Botanic Garden and now as a practicing garden designer. Its compact size and wealth of information makes this 'Pocket Guide' a handy and helpful companion.

Similar lists have been compiled as parts of larger reference books or in pamphlets of limited scope. This book suffers neither defect for in its small compass can be found not only all the common but many unusual landscape plants listed in every imaginable category.

The selection included in this English language edition has been specifically revised to include all the plants used in North American gardens plus a large number retained from the German edition which are still uncommon in our plantings. For each plant omitted from the German edition at least two new species have been added. 'Pocket Guide to Choosing Woody Ornamentals' will, it is hoped, be a useful addition to the libraries of garden designers, nurserymen, landscape contractors, architects and students as well as a helpful companion for the homeowner on a trip to the garden center.

As our world becomes 'smaller' it becomes increasingly vital to make the most of the outdoor space through effective landscape design. Good landscaping is no accident. It should be functional but have variety for interest and stability. This little book will be a valuable tool in the creation of tomorrow's landscape. I feel Herr Krüsmann had this idea in mind when he dedicated this book to young people. He wished to encourage them to become better aware of the varied and exciting world of plants.

Michael Epp

CONTENTS

5

Contents

FOREWORD

"The underlying idea of the first edition of this book has remained the same: a working reference for garden designers, landscape contractors, home gardeners and above all, young gardeners."

Dortmund-Brunninghausen
(Botanic Garden)
West Germany

Summer 1970   Gerd Krüssmann

So, Herr Krüssmann summed up the intent of this book. It is indeed a working reference of which I have made great use, first as an apprentice gardener at the Dortmund Botanic Garden and now as a practicing garden designer. Its compact size and wealth of information makes this 'Pocket Guide' a handy and helpful companion.

Similar lists have been compiled as parts of larger reference books or in pamphlets of limited scope. This book suffers neither defect for in its small compass can be found not only all the common but many unusual landscape plants listed in every imaginable category.

The selection included in this English language edition has been specifically revised to include all the plants used in North American gardens plus a large number retained from the German edition which are still uncommon in our plantings. For each plant omitted from the German edition at least two new species have been added. 'Pocket Guide to Choosing Woody Ornamentals' will, it is hoped, be a useful addition to the libraries of garden designers, nurserymen, landscape contractors, architects and students as well as a helpful companion for the homeowner on a trip to the garden center.

As our world becomes 'smaller' it becomes increasingly vital to make the most of the outdoor space through effective landscape design. Good landscaping is no accident. It should be functional but have variety for interest and stability. This little book will be a valuable tool in the creation of tomorrow's landscape. I feel Herr Krüsmann had this idea in mind when he dedicated this book to young people. He wished to encourage them to become better aware of the varied and exciting world of plants.

                                                        Michael Epp

INTRODUCTION

Guide to the Use of this Book

The book is divided into two parts.

Part I   contains plant material arranged according to properties; i.e. flowering time, flower color, foliage effect, fruit qualities, ornamental bark, growth habit, height etc.

Part II   focuses upon the uses that the same plants serve, arranged in groups according to specific soil types or situations; i.e. rock garden, street trees, industrial areas, windbreaks, etc.

Should plant material for a specific purpose be needed, it may be found in glance at the subject index, 'Where do I find plants for?' pp. 7-8

Legend to Abbreviations
— Specific location needed
  su = full sun   sh = shade needed or tolerated
  ss = semi-shade   u = good understory plant
Uncoded plants will thrive in sun or light shade.

— Specific soil types needed
  d = dry   S = sandy
  m = moist   Du = suitable for dune planting
  w = wet   H = prefers light humus
  A = alkaline
Uncoded plants thrive in normal garden soil.

— Growth habit
  cr = creeping
  cl = climbing
  wg = weeping
— Flower effects
  fl = ornamental flowers
  cf = suitable for cut flowers
  F = fragrant
— Leaf qualities
  of = ornamental foliage
  # = evergreen foliage
Colored foliage or fall coloration are not coded, but listed instead on p. 64.

— Fruiting effect
  fr = ornamental fruits
   e = edible fruits
Fruit colors listed on p. 74.

Hardiness is indicated by zone numbers corresponding to the U.S. Department of Agriculture hardiness map. A zone number is applied to each species, varieties are generally assumed to be of similar hardiness unless otherwise noted. Zone numbers will be found immediately following the plant names.

Where can I obtain the mentioned plants?

In choosing material from these lists the reader will naturally be concerned about availability. Many species may be found at or through your local garden center or nursery. However in many cases, the more uncommon plants will require some effort in locating. Besides the many nurseries limited to highly marketable items, there also exist those specializing in dwarf conifers, alpine plants, grafted varieties, rare species, etc. Organizations which may prove helpful in locating such material are: The American Association of Nurserymen, The Garden Club of America, The American Horticultural Society, International Plant Propagators Society, local botanic gardens, arboreta and universities. Communication with such groups will also enhance the awareness of the desire for new material.

I. THE PLANT PROPERTIES

1. Growth Habits
a. Columnar to Narrowly Conical

BROADLEAF

Acer platanoides 'Columnare' zone 3 su
— *rubrum* 'Armstrong' 3 su of
— *saccharum* 'Monumentale' 3 su of
Betula pendula 'Fastigiata' 2 su
Carpinus betulus 'Columnaris' (tall oval) 4 su-ss
— — 'Fastigiata' (='Pyramidalis') 4 su-ss
Crataegus monogyna 'Stricta' 4 su
— *phaenopyrum* 'Fastigiata' 4 su fl fr
Fagus sylvatica 'Fastigiata' (='Dawyckii') 4 su-ss
Gleditsia triacanthos 'Columnaris' 4 d su of
Ilex aquifolium 'Pyramidalis' 5 # su-sh fr
— *pernyi* 6 # su-sh
Koelreuteria paniculata 'Fastigiata' 5 fl su
Liriodendron tulipifera 'Fastigiatum' 5 su
Malus 'Van Eseltine' 4 su fl
Populus alba 'Pyramidalis' (='Bolleana') 3 su-ss
— *nigra* 'Italica' 4 su
— *simonii* 'Fastigiata' 2 su
— *tremula* 'Erecta' 2 su
Prunus avium 'Fastigiata' 3 K su-ss
— *sargentii* 'Columnaris' 4 fl
— *serrulata* 'Amanogawa' 5 K su-ss fl
Pyrus calleryana 'Bradford' 4 fl su
Quercus petraea 'Pyramidalis' 4 su
— *robur* 'Fastigiata' 5 su
Rhamnus frangula 'Columnaris' 2 su
Robinia pseudoacacia 'Erecta' 3 su fr
— — 'Pyramidalis' 3, su
Sophora japonica 'Fastigiata' 4 fl
Sorbus aucuparia 'Fastigiata' 2 su fl fr
Tilia platyphyllos 'Fastigiata' 3
Ulmus carpinifolia 'Dampieri' 4 su of
— 'Sarniensis'
— *glabra* 'Exoniensis' 4 su of
— *hollandica* 'Klemmer' 4 su

CONIFERS

Abies pinsapo 'Pyramidalis' 6 #, of

Rounded

Calocedrus decurrens 5 # su of
Cedrus atlantica 'Fastigiata' 6 # su of
Chamaecyparis lawsoniana 'Alumni' 5 # su-ss of
— — 'Columnaris' # su-ss
— — 'Ellwoodii' # su-ss of
— — 'Erecta Viridis' # su-ss of
Chamaecyparis lawsoniana 'Fletcheri' # su-ss of
— — 'Pottenii' # su-ss
— — 'Wisselii' # su-ss of
— *nootkatensis* 'Columnaris' 4 # su-ss
— *obtusa* 'Crippsii' 3 # su-ss of
Ginko biloba 'Fastigiata' 4 su of
              'Princeton Sentry'
Juniperus chinensis 'Columnaris' 4 #
— *communis* 'Compressa' (dwarf!) 2 # su
— — *var. hibernica* # su-ss
— — 'Suecica' # su-ss
— *virginiana* (form rounds with age) 2 # su-ss
— — 'Pyramidalis' # su-ss
— — 'Skyrocket' (most narrow) su-ss of
Metasequoia glyptostroboides 5
Picea abies 'Cupressina' 5 # su-ss
— *omorika* 4 # su
Pinus silvestris 'Fastigiata' 2 # su
— *strobus* 'Fastigiata' 3 #
Taxodium ascendens 'Nutans' 4 su of
— *distichum* 4 su of
Taxus baccata 'Stricta' (short needled) 6 # su-ss-sh of
— — 'Fastigiata' (and forms) # su-ss-sh
Thuja occidentalis 'Fastigiata' 2 # su-ss
— — 'Nigra' #
— — 'Techny' #

b. Oval to Rounded

BROADLEAF

Aesculus hippocastanum 'Umbraculifera'	zone 3 su	oval
Acer japonicum	5 su-ss	rounded, about 5m
— *palmatum*	5 su-ss of	about 5m high and wide
— — 'Dissectum'	su-ss of	about 3m high and wide
— — 'Ornatum' (Dissectum Atropurpurp.)	su-ss of	about 2m high and wide
— *platanoides* 'Globosum'	3 su-ss	attractive as a shrub
Catalpa bignonioides 'Nana'	4 su-ss	low round, very dense
Carpinus betulus 'Globosa'	4 su-ss	round, bushy
Cornus mas	4 su-sh fl fr	oval, dense
— *officinalis*	4 su-sh fl fr	wide oval, flowers earlier
Crataegus monogyna inermis 'Compacta'	4 su	low round, thornless
Fraxinus excelsior 'Globosa'	3 su	crown rounded

— *ornus* 'Globosa'	5 su	crown rounded
Magnolia soulangiana	5 su fl	wide round, large
— *stellata*	5 su fl	wide round, smaller
Malus arnoldiana	4 su fl fr	rounded
— *floribunda*	4 su fl	broad rounded
—*sargentii*	5 su fl fr	low rounded, 2m high
Morus alba 'Globosa	4 su	wide round, dense
Prunus cerasifera 'Pissardi'	su fl of	oval, foliage purple
Potentilla fruticosa (and varieties)	2 su fl	all more or less globose
Rhododendron impeditum	5 su fl	low cushion form
Robinia psuedoacacia 'Umbraculifera'	3 su	crown rounded
Salix purpurea 'Nana'	2 su	small round, fine texture
Viburnum opulus 'Nana'	3 su-sh	dense shrub, globose

CONIFERS

Chamaecyparis lawsoniana 'Minima Glauca'	5 # su-ss	wide oval, blue green
— *obtusa* 'Pygmaea'	3 # su-ss	Spherical, dark green
Picea abies 'Nidiformis'	4 # su	nest form
— — 'Gregoryana'	# su	(= Echiniformis)
— — 'Pumila Nigra'	# su	(= Pumila Glauca)
Pinus densiflora 'Umbraculifera'	4 # su	wide, umbrella shaped
— *mugo mughus*	2 # su	
— *mugo pumilio*	2 # su	cushion form
— *strobus* 'Nana'	3 # su	
Thuja occidentalis 'Globosa'	2 # su-ss	
— — 'Woodwardi'	# su-ss	
Tsuga canadensis 'Globosa'	4 # su-ss	

c. Weeping Habit

BROADLEAF

Acer saccharinum 'Wieri' zone 3 su of
Alnus incana 'Pendula' 2 su
Betula pendula 'Gracilis' (finely branched) 2 su of
— — 'Tristis' (upright, tips weeping) su
— — 'Youngii' (Prostrate, must be staked) su
Buddleia alternifolia, (wide branching) 5 su fl
Caragana arborescens 'Pendula' 2 su fl
Cornus florida 'Pendula' 4 su-ss fl
Corylus avellana 'Pendula' 4 su-ss
Cotoneaster watereri 'Pendulus' 5 su fr cr
— *salicifolius floccocus* (branches wide arching) 6 # su fr
Fagus sylvatica 'Pendula' (strong grower, green) 4 su
— — 'Pendula Purpurea' (sparse branching, red) su of
Forsythia suspensa 5 su-ss fl
Fraxinus excelsior 'Diversifolia Pendula' 3 su of

Weeping

Gleditsia triacanthos 'Bujotii'
  (very finely branched, rare) zone|4 su of
Jasminum nudiflorum 5 su-ss fl cr
Laburnum alpinum 'Pendulum'
  (branches sharply weeping) 4 su
Malus 'Echtermeyer' 4 su fl fr
— 'Red Jade' 4 su fl fr
Morus alba 'Pendula' 4 su
Pyrus salicifolia 4 su of
Populus tremula 'Pendula' 2 su
— *tremuloides* 'Pendula' 1 su
Prunus cerasifera 'Pendula' 4 A su fl fr e
— *mahaleb* 'Pendula' 6 A su
— *mume* 'Pendula' 6 su fl
— *serrulata* 'Kiku-shidare-sakura' 5 A fl su
— *subhirtella* 'Pendula' (and forms) 5 A su fl
— *yedoensis* 'perpendens' 5 A su fl
— *persica* 'Windle Weeping' 4 A fl fr su
Quercus robur 'Pendula' 5 su
Rosa, as weeping varieties grafted on standards. su
Salix alba 'Tristis' (='Vitellina Pendula) 2 su of
— *babylonica* 6 su of
— *caprea* 'Pendula' 4 su
— *elegantissima* 4 su of
— *purpurea* 'Pendula' 3 su
Sophora japonica 'Pendula' 4 su of
Sorbus aucuparia 'Pendula' 2 su of fl fr
Tilia petiolaris (branch tips pendulous) 5 su
Ulmus glabra 'Camperdownii' 4 su
— — 'Pendula' (crown wide umbrella form) su

CONIFERS

Cedrus atlantica 'pendula Glauca' zone 6 # su
— *deodar* 'Pendula' 6 # su
Cedrus libani 'Pendula' 5 # su cr
Chamaecyparis lawsoniana 'Pendula' 5 # su-ss of
— — 'Oregon Blue' 6 # su-ss of
— *nootkatensis* 'Pendula'
  (beautiful weeping conifer) 4 # su-ss of
— *pisifera* 'Nana' 3 # su of
— — 'Nana Aurea' # su of
Gingko biloba 'Pendula' (umbrealla form) 4 su
Juniperus communis 'Oblongo-pendula' 2 # su
— *virginiana* 'Pendula' 2 # su
Larix decidua 'Pendula' 2 su
— *kaempferi* 'Pendula' 7 su
Picea abies 'Pendula' 5 su
— *breweriana*
  (branches hang like a horses mane) 5 # su of
— *pungens* 'Pendens' 2 # su
— — *glauca* 'Pendula' # su

14

Pinus strobus 'Pendula' 3 # su
Pseudotsuga menziesii 'Pendula' 5 # su
Sequoiadendron giganteum 'Pendula' 6 # su
Taxus baccata 'Dovastoniana'
  (branches horizontal, green) 6 # su-ss of
— — 'Dovastoniana Aureovariegata' (as above, yellow) # su-ss of

d. Dwarf Habit
(Broadleaf, see p. 106)

CONIFERS

I. Creeping

Juniperus communis				
'Hornbrookii'	zone 2	green	1—3m wide	30—60cm high
— — 'Repanda'		deep green	1m "	30—50cm "
— *horizontalis*				
'Douglasii'	3	blue	2—3m "	30—50cm "
— — 'Glauca'		blue	2—3m "	10—20cm "
— — 'Plumosa'		blue-green	2—3m "	20—30cm "
— — 'Prostrata'		blue	3—4m "	20—30cm "
— procumbens	4	green	2—3m "	30—40cm "
— — 'Nana'		green	1m "	20—30cm "
— sabina				
'Tamariscifolia'	4	blue-green	1—2m "	50—100cm "
Picea abies 'Repens'	3	green	1—2m "	40—50cm "
Pinus densiflora				
'Pendula'	4	green	1—2m "	40—50cm "
— *mugo pumilio*	2	green	1—2m "	50—100cm "

II. Dwarf Conifers, less than 1m high

Abies balsamea				
'Nana'	zone 5	globular	green	to 1m
Cedrus libani 'Nana'	6	globular	green	to 1m
Chamaecyparis				
lawsoniana 'Minima'	5	wide, round	green	to 1m
— *obtusa* 'Coralliformis'	3	egg shape	green	
— — 'Lycopodioides Aurea'		bushy	bright yellow	to 1m
— — 'Mariesii'		conical	bright yellow	to 1m
— — 'Nana'		wide, low	green	to 50cm
— *pisifera* 'Plumosa				
Compressa'	3	bushy	green	50—60cm
— — 'Nana'		cushion form	green	30—40 cm
— — 'Nana Variegata'		cushion form	yellow	30—40cm
Cryptomeria				
Japonica 'Globosa				
Nana'	5	hemispherical	green	to 1m
— — 'Vilmoriana'	5	hemispherical	green	60—80cm
Juniperus chinensis				
sargentii	4	wide	green	40—60m

Dwarf

—— *sargentii* 'Glauca'	4	wide	blue-green	40—60cm
— *communis* 'Depressa'	2	wide	blue-green	to 1m
—— 'Depressa Aurea'	2	wide	yellow-green	80—100cm
—— 'Compressa'		columnar	blue	to 60cm
—— *montana* (= nana)		wide	light green	to 80cm
— *virginiana* 'Globosa'	2	spherical	green	80 cm
Picea abies				
'Gregoryana'	5	spherical	green	60—80cm
— *glauca* 'Echiniformis'	2	round, flat topped	blue-gray	30—40cm
— *pungens* 'Glauca Globosa'	2	round, flat topped	light blue	50—80cm
Taxus baccata				
'Repandens' zone	5	wide, low	deep green	60cm
—— Repandens Aurea'		very wide	yellow	50cm
Thujopsis dolobrata				
'Nana'	6	wide	green	80—100cm
Thuja occidentalis				
'Tiny Tim'	4	globular	green	50—100cm

III. Dwarf Conifers, 1—2m and more

Chamaecyparis lawsoniana				
'Forsteckensis' zone	5	spherical	blue-green	1.2m
—— 'Minima Glauca'		broadly conical	blue-green	1.3m
— *obtusa*				
'Lycopodioides'	3	bushy	green	2m
—— 'Nana Aurea'		conical	yellow	2m
—— 'Nana Gracilis'		conical	deep green	2m
—— 'Pygmaea'		rounded	green	1.5m
—— 'Tetragona Aurea'		conical	yellow	2m
— *pisifera*				
'Filifera Nana'	3	conical	green	2m
—— 'Filifera Aurea'		conical	yellow	1.5m
Cryptomeria japonica				
'Jindai-sugi'	5	conical	green	2m
—— 'Dacrydioides'		bushy	green	2×2m
Juniperus chinensis				
'Pfitzeriana'	4	bushy	green	2×4m
Juniperus chinensis	4			
'Pfitzeriana Aurea'		bushy	yellow-green	2×2m
—— 'Pfitzeriana Glauca'		bushy	blue-green	1.5m
—— 'Pfitzeriana Compacta'		bushy	blue-green	1×1m
—— 'Old Gold'		bushy	yellow-green	1.5m
—— 'Plumosa'		bushy	green	1.5m
—— 'Plumosa Aurea'		bushy	yellow-green	1.5m
—— 'Blaauwi'		bushy	blue-green	2m
—— 'Hetzii'		upright	blue-green	2—3m
— *sabina*	4	broad	green	1.5
— *squamata* 'Meyeri'	4	upright	blue	2—5m
—— *wilsonii*		upright	blue-green	to 2m

— *virginiana*				
'Grey Owl'	2	broad	blue-green	to 1.5m
Picea abies				
'Compacta'	5	conical	green	2m
— — 'Nidiformis'		nest form	green	1—2m
— — 'Pumila Nigra'		hemispherical	green	1m
— — 'Pygmaea'		conical	green	1.5m
— — 'Remontii'		conical	green	2m
— *glauca* 'Conica'	2	conical	bright green	2m and more
— *omorika* 'Nana'	4	broadly conical	green	2m
— *orientalis* 'Gracilis'	5	egg shape	deep green	2m
Pinus silvestris				
'Argentea Compacta'	2	conical	blue	to 2m
— — 'Watereri'		rounded	blue	2—4m
— — 'Glauca Nana'		globose	blue-green	2—4m
— *strobus* 'Nana'	3	flat round	blue-green	1m
Taxus baccata				
'Nissens Corona'	6	flat round	bright green	1.5m
— — 'Nissens President'		broad	deep green	2m
— — 'Semperaurea'		twisting upright	yellow	1.5—2m
— — 'Washingtonii'		broad, open	yellow-green	1.5—2m
— *cuspidata* 'Nana'	4	irregular	deep green	1.5—2m
Taxus media				
'Hatfieldii'	2	conical	green	2m
— — 'Hicksii'		columnar	green	2m
— — 'Everlow'		broad	bright green	1.2m
Thuja occidentalis				
'Filiformis'	2	wide, round	green	1.5m
— — 'Globosa'		spherical	green	2m
— — 'Ohlendorffii'		spherical	brwn-green	1.5m
— — 'Recurva Nana'		spherical	green	1.2m
— — 'Rheingold'		conical	yellow and brown	1.5m
— — 'Umbraculifera'		rounded	green	1.5m
Tsuga canadensis				
'Jeddeloh'	4	nest form	green	1m
— — 'Nana'		globular	green	1m

e. Rapid Growing

DECIDUOUS

Acer negundo zone 2 su
— *platanoides* 3 su
— *psuedoplatanus* 5 su
— *rubrum* 3 su
— *saccharinum* 3 su
Aesculus hippocastanum 3 su fl of
Ailanthus altissima 4 su

Catalpa bignonioides 4 fl
Corylus colurna 4 su
Eleagnus angustifolia 2 su of
Fagus silvatica 4 su-ss of
Fraxinus americana 3 su of
— *excelsior* 3 su of
    sylvanica 3 su

Slow Growing

Betula, most spp.
Gleditsia triacanthos **4 su of**

Juglans nigra **4 of**
Liriodendron
tulipifera **4 su of**
Magnolia acuminata **4 of fl**
— *obovata* **5 of fl**
— *tripetala* **5 of fl**
Malus, (most forms) **fl fr e**
Paulownia tomentosa **5 of fl**
Populus, (most forms)
Platanus **spp.**
Prunus avium **3 fl**
— *cerasifera* **4 fl**
— *padus* **3 fl**
— *serotina* **3 fl fr**

— *serrulata*
(and varieties) **3 fl**
Pterostyrax hispida **5 fl**
Quercus palustris **4 su**
— *rubra* **4 su**
Robinia psuedoacacia **3 fl**
Salix, (most forms)
Sambucus nigra **5 of fl fr**
Sorbus aucuparia **2 of fl fr**
Sophora japonica **4 fl**
Tilia europaea **3 su**
— *platyphylla* **3 su**
Ulmus, (most forms)

CONIFEROUS

Abies grandis **zone 6# of**
— *concolor lowiana* **4 # of**
— *nordmaniana* **4 # of**
Cedrus atlantica **6 # of**
Cryptomeria japonica **5 # of**
Larix decidua **2 of**
— *kaempferi* **7 of**
Metasequoia glypto. **5 of**
Picea abies **5 #**
— *omorika* **4 # of**

Pinus nigra **4 #**
— *silvestris* **2 #**
— *strobus* **3 #**
Psuedotsuga menziesii **5 #**
Sequoiadendron giganteum **6 #, of**
Thuja plicata **5 #**
— *occidentalis* **2 #**
Tsuga canadensis **4 #**
— *heterophylla* **6 #**

f. Slow Growing Plants

BROADLEAF

Acer griseum **zone 5 of**
— *nikoense* **5 of**
— *palmatum*, (and forms) **5 of**
— *saccharum* **3 of**
Betula medwediewii **4 ot**
Chaenomeles japonica **4 fl fr**
Crataegus lavallei **4 of fl fr**
— *monogyna* **'Compacta' 4 of**
— *orientalis* **5 of fr**

Fraxinus ornus **5 fl**
Gymnocladus dioecus **4 of**
Ilex, most **# fr of**
Ligustrum vulgare
'Lodense' **4 of**

Liquidambar styraciflua **5 of**
Maackia amurensis **4 fl**
Parrotia persica **5 fl**
Phellodendron amurense **3 su**
Quercus, **most**
Sorbus koehneana **5 of fr**
— *prattii* **5 of fr**
— *vilmorinii* **5 of fr**
Syringa reticulata
(— *amurensis japonica*) **4 fl**
— *microphylla* **4 of fl**
— *pinnatifolia* **5 of fl**
Tilia cordata **3 of su**

Lonicera xylosteum
'Claveyi' 4
Corylus colurna 4 su

Ulmus carpinifolia
(and types— 4 su
— *parvifolia* 5 of su
— *pumila* 4

EVERGREEN

all dwarf conifers # of
Abies, many types # of
— *koreana* 5 # of fr
— *pinsapo* 6 # of
Chamaecyparis obtusa 3 # of
Picea pungens 2 # of

Pinus cembra 4 #
— *pumila* 4 #
Sciadopitys verticillata 5 # of
Taxus cuspidata 4 #
Thuja koraiensis 5 of #

g. Plants with Special Architectural Effects

Acer rufinerve, zone 5 Bark green with white stripes
— *palmatum* 'Dissectum', 5 grows wide, low, foliage fine textured
Aralia elata, 3 stout thorny stems, huge leaves
Cornus alternifolia, 4 rounded tree, fine horizontal branching
Corylus avellana 'Contorta', 3 cork-screw branching, to 3m
Crataegus punctata 'Ohio Pioneer', 4 low, horizontal head
Decaisnea fargesii, 6 large pinnate leaves, fruit a blue pod
Eleagnus commutata, 4 strictly upright, foliage silver
— *ebbingei*, 6 shrub of medium height, foliage glossy green and silver
— *pungens*, 7 upper leaf green and yellow, underside silver
Euonymus alatus, 3 corky branches, bright red fall foliage
— *europaeus* 'Aldenhamensis'. 3 as above in tree form, red-orange fruit capsules
Fagus silvatica 'Laciniata', 4 foliage finely cut
— — 'Pendula', growth inconsistent, broad weeping
Juniperus virginiana 'Skyrocket', 2 super narrow column, blue
Malus 'Van Eseltine', 4 columnar, full pink flowers
— 'Red Jade', low, wide branching, weeping, red fruits
Prunus maackii, 2 bark always bright yellow-orange
— *serrula*, 5 bark a highly polished red-brown
— *serrulata* 'Amanogawa', 5 columnar, flowers bright pink
— *subhirtella* 'Autumnalis', 5 blooms Nov.—December
— *yedoensis*, 5 blooms early April, loose open habit
Quercus robur 'Pendula', 5 exceptional for arbors
Rhus typhina 'Dissecta', 5 spreads wide, bright red fall color
Salix matsudana 'Tortuosa', 4 twisting branches, tall oval tree
— *sachalinense* 'Sekka', 4 wide shrub, branch tips clustered and fused
Ulmus glabra 'Camperdownii', 4 "Arbor Elm", dome shaped crown
— — 'Pendula', crown broad umbrella shape

h. Vines and Climbers

Actinidia arguta, 4 white fl su-ss fr 3
— *chinensis*, 7 white fl su-ss fr of e
— *kolomikta*, 4 white fl su-ss fr of
— *polygama*, 4 white fl su-ss fr e F

Vines & Climbers

Akebia quinata, 4 purple fl su-ss
Ampelopsis aconitifolia, 4 su-ss fr
— *arborea*, 7, of
— *brevipedunculata* 'Elegans', 4 su-ss of
Aristolchia macrophylla, 4 su-ss of
Bignonia capreolata, 6 orange-red fl of #
Celastus orbiculata, 4 yellow-red fr su-ss
— *scandens*, 2 yellow-red fr su-ss
Campsis grandiflora, 7 red fl su
— *radicans*, 4 red fl su
— x *tagliabuana* 'Madame Galen', 4 red fl su
— 'Yellow Trumpet', 4 yellow fl su
Cissus incisa, 8
Clematis, small flowered types
— *alpina*, 4 violet fl su-sh
— *koreana*, 5 lilac to yellow fl su-ss
— *montana*, 5 white fl su-ss
— — 'Grandiflora', white fl su-ss
— — 'Rubens', pink fl su-ss
— — 'Tetrarose', pink, larger flowers su-ss
— *orientalis*, 4 yellow fl su-ss
— *paniculata*, 5 white fl su-ss
— *tangutica*, 5 yellow fl su-ss
— *rehderiana*, 4 bright yellow fl su-ss
— *vitalba*, 4 white fl su-sh
— — 'Kermesiana', wine red fl su-ss
— — 'Venosa', violet venation fl su-ss
Clematis, large flowered types
— 'Barbara Dibley', violet red fl su-ss
— 'Belle of Woking', double blue fl su-ss
— 'Crimson King', wine red fl su-ss
— 'Duchess of Edinburgh', double white fl su-ss
— *durandii*, violet-blue, cross form fl su-ss
— 'Ernest Markham', dark red fl su-ss
— 'Gypsy Queen', dark purple fl su-ss
— 'Henryi', white fl su-ss
— 'Huldine', white fl su-ss
— 'Jackmanii', violet-blue fl su-ss
— 'Jackmanii Superba', violet-purple fl su-ss
— 'Lady BettyBalfour', deep purple fl su-ss
— 'Lady Northcliffe', lavender fl su-ss
— 'Lincoln Star', pink center, white margin fl su-ss
— 'Mme Baron-Veillard', lilac-pink fl su-ss
— 'Mm Le Coultre', white fl su-ss
— 'M. Koster', lilac-pink fl su-ss
— 'Nelly Moser', lilac-pink, red band fl su-ss
— 'President', violet-blue fl su-ss
— 'Ramona', large blue fl su-ss
— 'Star of India', plum purple, red band fl su-ss
— 'Ville de Lyon', rich crimson (Carmine) fl su-ss
— 'Will Goodwin', sky blue, yellow stamens fl su-ss
Euonymus fortunei 'Carrierei', 5 # su-sh of

— — 'Coloratus', u su-sh of
— — 'Gracilis', # white venation of su-sh
— — *radicans*, 5 # u su-sh
— — 'Silver Gem', whitish # of su-sh
— — 'Vegetus', # of su-sh
— *obovatus*, 3 fr of su
Hedera colchica, 5 # u ss-sh of
— *canariensis*, 7 # of fr
— *helix*, 5 # u ss-sh
Hydrangea anomala petiolaris, 4 u fl ss-sh
Jasminum beesianum, 6 pink fl ss
— *mesnyi*, 8 yellow fl
— *nudiflorum*, 5 (winter blooming) yellow fl su-sh
— *officinale*, 7 white fl F
— *stephanense*, 6 pink fl su-ss
Kadsura japonica, 7 yellow-white fl
Lonicera brownii, 5 orange fl su-ss
— *caprifolium*, 5 cream fl su-sh
— *flava*, 5 yellow-orange fl
— *heckrotti*, 5 purple and yellow fl su-ss
— *henryi*, 4 # su-sh
— *japonica*, 4 u white fl su-ss
— *sempervirens*, 3 orange to scarlet fl
Lonicera tellmaniana, 5 yellow-orange fl su-ss
Lycium halimifolium, 4 lilac-purple fl
Menispermum canadense 4 of su-sh
Muehlenbeckia complexa, 5
Parthenocissus quinquefolia, 3 of su-sh
— — 'Engelmanii', of su-sh
— *henryana*, 8 of sh
— *heptaphylla*, 8
— *tricuspidata*, 4 of su-ss
— — 'Veitchii', of su-ss
Passiflora caerulea, 7—8 white to blue fl
Periploca graeca, 8 su
Pileostegia viburnoides, 7 white fl
Polygonum aubertii, 4 pure white fl su
Pueraria lobata, 6 (invasive)
Rosa, climbers see p. 63
Rubus henryi, 6 # of su-sh
— — *bambusarium*, 6 # of ss-sh
Schisandra propinqua, 8 orange fl fr of #
Schizophragma hydrangeoides, 6 fl su-sh
Smilax megalanta, 7 fr
— *rotundifolia*, 4 fr
Trachelospermum asiaticum, 7 yellow-white fl
Vitis coignetiae, 5 su of
— *riparia* (=odoratissima), 2 of su-sh
— *vinifera* 'Purpurea', 4 of su
Wisteria floribunda, 4 lilac, 50cm long fl su-ss
— *sinensis*, 5 lilac, 15-30 cm long fl su-ss

2. Ornamental Bark Effects

GREEN

Acer capillipes	zone 6	of fr	green with white stripes
— *davidii*	6	of	as above, glossy in winter
— *grosseri*	6	of	green, striped white
— *pensylvanicum*	3	of	as above
— *rufinerve*	5	of	bluish-white stripes when young, greening with age
Cytisus praecox	5	fl	gray-green
— *scoparius* (and types)	5	fl	dark green
Euonymus alatus	3	of fr	bright green, corky wings
Genista tinctoria	2	fl	dark green
Jasminum nudiflorum	5	fl	dark green, flowers yellow in winter
Kerria japonica 'Plenaflora'	4	fl	dark green
Laburnum x watereri	5	fl	bright green
Poncirus trifoliata	6	fl fr	dark green
Rosa wichuriana	5	fl	bright green
Sophora japonica	4	fl	very dark green
Spartium junceum	7	fl	deep green
Ulex europaea	6	fl	dark green thorns and stems
Salix blanda	4		young branches green

YELLOW TO ORANGE

Alnus incana 'Aurea'	2	of	red-orange
Betula albo sinensis	5		bright orange red exfoliating
Cornus stolonifera 'Flaviramea'	2	fl fr	striking yellow-green
Corylus avellana 'Aurea'	3	of	young twigs orange
Fraxinus excelsior 'Aurea'	3	of	young branches yellow, sparse and open
Fraxinus excelsior 'Jaspidea'	3	of	strong grower, branches yellow
Prunus maackii	2		bark consistent yellow-orange
Salix alba 'Tristis'	2		bright yellow

RED

Acer cappadocicum	5-6	of	red, glossy sometimes glaucous
— *griseum*	5	of	fine twigged, cinnamon red flaking bark
— *palmatum*	5	of	young branches dark red, fine textured
Arbutus menziesii	7	fl	smooth muscled, bright red trunk
Cornus alba	2	fl fr	red
— — 'Siberica'		fl fr	coral red, most attractive

— *stolonifera*	2	fl fr	dark brown-red
Itea virginica	5	fl	bright red
Lonicera coerulea	6	fl fr	red
Pinus densiflora	4	#	orange-red
— *resinosa*	2	#	reddish brown
— *sylvestris*	2	#	red on older branches
Prunus serrula	5		glossy brown-red, outstanding!
— *sargentii*	4	fl	dark red
Rosa gallica	5	fl	red
— *cinnamomea*	5	fl	red
Stephanandra tanakae	6	of fl	red-brown

BLACK

Cornus alba			
'Kesselringii'	2	fl fr	blackish-red
Eleagnus angustifolia	2	of	black-brown
Rhus typhina	5	of fr	blackish-red densely hairy
Syringa reticulata	4	fl	black-red, cherry bark
Tamarix parviflora	4	fl of	black-brown
— *tetrandra*	6	fl of	black-brown

GRAY

Acer rubrum	3		bright silver-gray
Amelanchier canadensis	4	fl fr of	light gray
Carpinus **spp.**			dark gray, smooth bark
Crataegus, many spp.		fl fr	lead gray, thorny
Eleagnus commutata	4	of	silver-gray, later darker gray
— *umbellata*	3	of	gray
Fagus spp.			silver gray on older trunks
Magnolia soulangiana	5	fl	silver gray
Populus tremula	2	of	gray-green
— *tremuloides*	1	of	gray-green
— *alba* 'Pyramidalis'	3	of	gray-green
Sorbus, most spp.		fl fr	gray, not exceptional

WHITE

Acer floridanum	9		very light, smooth
Betula, **see list on p. 32**			
Berberis dictyophylla	6	fl of	bluish-white bloom
Populus alba	3	of	snow white tomentum
Rhus glabra	2	fl of fr	bluish-white bloom on young branches
Rubus biflorus	4	of	chalk white
— *cockburnianus*	4	of	bluish-white bloom
— *tibetanus*	4	of	bluish-white bloom
Salix acutifolia	4	of fl	red with dense white bloom
— — 'Pendulifolia'		of fl	orange-red, white bloom
— *daphnoides*	4	of fl	red, dense blue-white bloom
— *irrorata*	4	fl	black-brown, white bloom

Birches

PEELING BARK (except Birches)

Acer griseum	zone 5	of	cinnamon brown, peeling in fine thin rolls
Prunus maackii	2	fl	bright yellow-orange, as if polished, thinly peeling
— serrula	5	fl fr	golden red-brown, highly polished, most beautiful!
Rosa roxburghii	5	fl fr	peeling and prickly
Viburnum molle	3	fl	peeling in large bits

FLAKING, PATCHY BARK

Arbutus unedo	zone 7	fl	bright red, flaky
Eucalyptus spp.			exfoliating in strips exposing lighter, inner bark
Parrotia persica	5	of fl	dappled, light and dark gray-green
Pinus bungeana	4	of #	in autumn a pattern of white, green, gray and red, outstanding!
— silvestris	2	of #	fox red, flaky
Platanus acerifolia	4	of	large patches of gray and and greenish white
— orientalis	6	of	checkered in small flaking patches, as with pear trees
Stewartia chinensis	5	of fl	older wood gray-green without bark
— pseudo-camellia	5	of fl	red and gray checked
Rhododendron campanulatum	5	fl #	older stems light gray, without bark

BIRCHES (Betula)

(Due to extensive hybridization within the genus Betula, the colors described are those most typical of the species. Those without ornamental bark have been omitted.)

albosinensis	of	zone 5	bright orange or simply gray
costata	of	5	gray-brown
davurica	of	4	gray as cork
ermanii	of	5	reddish gray to near white
grossa	of	5	almost black
lenta	of	3	red brown, cherrylike
lutea	of	3	golden brown
maximowicziana	of	5	orange or more gray to cream
nigra	of	4	black-brown flaky, twigs yellow-brown
papyrifera	of	2	bright white, young bark brown
pendula	of	2	white with black markings
platyphylla	of	5	white, brown at first

populifolia		3	chalk white, often multistemmed
pubescens		2	white
utilis	of	7	white and deep brown

CORKY BARK

Corylus colurna	of	4	thick, bright gray bark
Euonymus alatus	of fr	3	having corky wings on young twigs
— *phellomanus*	of fr	4	cork wings wider
Liquidambar styraciflua	of	5	young twigs and branches with corky bark
Phellodendron amurense	of fr	3	trunk bright gray, cork thick, deeply grooved
Ulmus carpinifolia suberosa		4	thick corky wings on branches and young twigs
Quercus suber		8	produces cork of economic use

CONSPICUOUS THORNS

Aralia elata	of fr	zone 3	branches stout with strong thorns
Acanthopanax sieboldianus	of	4	thorns numerous, attractive foliage
Berberis actinacantha	of #	6	thorns numerous, flat
— *julianae*	#	5	thorns long and stout
— *koreana*	of	5	thorns large, flat
Crataegus crusgalli	of fl	4	thorns strong, 14cm long
— *lavallei*	fr of fl	4	thorns stout and strong
Genista hispanica	fl	6	thorns green and small, but thick
Gleditsia spp.	of		red-brown thorns, very numerous, 10—20cm
Hemiptelea davidii	of	6	stout thorns to 10cm long
Kalopanax pictus	of	4	branches contain many short stout prickles
Maclura pomifera		4	thorns numerous, short
Malus transitoria	fr of	6	densely thorny on short branches
Paliurus spina-christi	fl of fr	7	numerous pairs of unequal thorns
Poncirus trifoliata	fl of fr	6	thorns wide, dark green
Prunus spinosa	fr	4	short black branches densely thorny
Rosa omeiensis	fl fr	4	thorns 2—3cm wide, very thick
— — *pteracantha*	fl fr	6	thorns 3—4 cm wide
— *pteragonis*	fl fr	6	young thorns red-brown, 3—5 cm wide
Ulex europaeus	fl	6	twigs and thorns grass green

3. Flowering Times

a. Table of the Major

	white	yellow	red
March	*Prunus, Magnolia*	*Cornus mas, Salix Forsythia, Corylus Corylopsis, Alnus Jasminum*	*Erica carnea Acer rubrum*
April	*Prunus, Magnolia, Amelanchier, Spirea, Pieris*	as March, also *Mahonia, Ribes*	*Ribes, Prunus Malus, Erica Chaenomeles*
May	*Prunus, Amelanchier, Malus, Pyrus, Deutzia, Crataegus Pieris, Viburnum, Syringa, Chionanthus, Halesia, Exochorda, Spirea*	*Mahonia, Berberis Cytisus, Caragana, Potentilla, Laburnum, Rhododendron, Azalea*	*Malus, Crataegus Syringa, Azalea, Tamarix, Rhododen-dron, Paeonia, Weigela*
June	*Philadelphus, Rosa Deutzia, Spirea, Robinia, Cornus*	*Rosa, Cytisus, Lonicera, Potentilla*	*Rosa, Lonicera, Clematis*
July	*Hydrangea, Spirea, Rosa, Hibiscus Aesculus, Clematis*	*Rosa, Hypericum Potentilla*	*Hydrangea, Rosa, Spirea, Fuchsia*
August	*Rosa, Spirea Hydrangea, Hibiscus, Buddleia, Polygonum, Clethra*	*Rosa, Hypericum, Potentilla*	*Indigofera, Rosa Spirea, Buddleia, Campsis, Lespedeza, Calluna*
September	*Rosa, Hydrangea*	*Rosa, Potentilla*	*Rosa, Calluna*
October		*Rosa, Hamamelis Potentilla*	*Rosa*
Nov.—Dec.		*Jasminum*	late *Rosa*
Jan-Feb.		*Hamamelis, Jasminum*	*Hamamelis, Parrotia*

and Colors

Flowering Plants (in Zone 6)

pink	purple	blue	
Erica carnea, Daphne, Magnolia Prunus	Rhododendron praecox, **Azaleas**		March
as March, plus Tamarix, Lonicera, Rhododendron, Chaenomeles	as March, plus Daphne genkwa	Rhododendron	April
Malus, Crataegus Syringa, **Azaleas,** Tamarix, Paeonia, Rhododendron, Viburnum, Weigela	Rhododendron, Syringa, Malus, Wisteria, Weigela	Rhododendron, Syringa, Wisteria, Lithospermum	May
Rosa, Robinia, Lonicera	Rosa, Weigela Clematis	Rhododendron, Clematis	June
Hydrangea, Spirea, Rosa	Clematis	Hydrangea, Clematis	July
Hibiscus, Rosa, Buddleia, Calluna	Hibiscus, Buddleia, Calluna	Hibiscus, Perovskia, Caryopteris, Buddleia	August
Rosa, Calluna	Calluna	Caryopteris	September
Rosa, Camellia	Calluna		October
late Rosa			Nov.—Dec.
Erica carnea 'Winter Beauty'	Rhododendron mucronulatum		Jan.—Feb.

Lasting Flowers

b. Flowering Calendar of the Lasting Flowers

This category includes those plants with more than one flowering period and those with flowers opening one after another. Months in bloom are indicated by number following the species.

Species	4	5	6	7	8	9	10	11	notes	zone	color
Rubus spectabilis	4	5	6							zone 5	bright red
Ulex europaeus	4	5				9	10			6	yellow
Clematis alpina		5	6	7						4	blue
— *jackmanii* (and types)				7	8	9	10			5	blue, lilac purple
— *lanuginosa* (and types)		5		7	8	9	10			5	white, lilac
— *patens* (and types)		5	6	7	8					5	blue, lilac
Colutea all		5	6	7	8				fr		yellow, brown
Coronilla emerus		5	6	7	8	9	10			4	yellow
Escallonia, all		5	6	7	8						pink, red, white
Kerria japonica 'Plena'		5	6	7	8	9			cf	4	golden yellow
Lycium, all		5	6	7	8	9			fr		lilac red
Potentilla fruticosa		5	6	7	8	9	10		cf	2	yellow, white, red, orange
Robinia hispida		5	6	7	8					5	pink
Rubus parviflorus		5	6	7						4	white
Spartium junceum		5	6	7	8	9				7	bright yellow
Vinca minor		5	6	7	8	9			sh cr #	4	blue
Abelia grandiflora			6	7	8	9	10		cf #	5	pink-white
Diervilla, all			6	7	8				sh		bright yellow
Genista tinctoria			6	7	8				cf	2	yellow
Hydrangea arborescens 'Grandiflora'			6	7	8	9			cf	4	white
Jasminum officinale			6	7	8	9			F	7	white
Robinia holdtii britzensis			6		8	9				5	bright pink
— *psuedoacacia* 'Semperflorens'			6	7	8	9				3	white
Rosa, see list p. 60			6	7	8	9	10	11	fr F cf		pink, red white, yellow
Rubus odoratus			6	7	8				F	3	purple
Spirea bumalda			6	7	8				cf	5	red, pink
— *menziesii*			6	7	8				cf	5	bright red
— *veitchii*			6	7	8				cf	5	white
Buddleia davidii (and types)				7	8	9			cf	5	white, lilac red, blue
Cephalanthus occidentalis				7	8	9				4	white

28

Campsis radicans	7	8	9	.	.	.	.	.	zone 4	red
Clethra, all	7	8	9	.	.	.	.			white
Fuchsia gracilis	7	8	9	10	.	.	.		7	red
Hypericum patulum (and types)	7	8	9	10	.	.	.	.	6	yellow
Indigofera gerardiana	7	8	9	.	.	.	.	.	5	purple
Lespedeza bicolor	7	8	9	.	.	.	.	.	4	violet-red
— thunbergii	7	8	9	10					4	violet-red
Polygonum aubertii	7	8	9	.	.	.	.	.	4	white
Caryopteris clandonensis	.	8	9	.	.	.	.	.	5	blue
Elsholtzia stauntonii	.	.	9	10	.	.	.		4	blue-purple
Jasminum nudiflorum	.	.	.	.	11	12	1—3		5	yellow
Erica carnea (and types)	4	.	.	.	.	12	1—3		5	pink, white, red

c. Flowering Calendar

Ordered alphabetically and chronologically for Zone 6.

Acer negundo	3	4	.	.	.	.	.	.	zone 2		yellow-green
— rubrum	3	4	.	.	.	.	.	.		3	red
Alnus, all	3	4	5	.	.	.	.	.	fr		catkins
Chaenomeles japonica	3	4	.	.	.	.	.	.	fr cf	4	brick red
— speciosa (and types)	3	4	.	.	.	.	.	.	fr cf	4	red, pink, white
Cornus mas	3	4	.	.	.	.	.	.	fr	4	yellow
— officinalis	3	4	.	.	.	.	.	.		4	yellow, two weeks earlier
Corylopsis, all	3	4	.	.	.	.	.	.	cf		bright yellow
Daphne mesereum	3	.	.	.	.	.	.	.	fr F	4	purple
— — 'Album'	3	.	.	.	.	.	.	.	fr F	4	white
Forsythia ovata	3	4	.	.	.	.	.	.	cf	4	yellow
Magnolia stellata	3	4	.	.	.	.	.	.	cf	5	white
Parrotia persica	3	4	.	.	.	.	.	.	of cf	5	brown and red
Pieris floribunda	3	4	.	.	.	.	.	.	cf of #	4	white
— japonica	3	4	5	.	.	.	.	.	cf of #	5	white
Prunus dulcis	3	4	.	.	.	.	.	.	fr e	4	pink-white
Prunus davidiana	3	.	.	.	.	.	.	.	cf	6	pink
— 'Okame'	3	4	.	.	.	.	.	.		6	pink
— subhirtella	3	4	.	.	.	.	.	.	cf	5	white with pink
Salix acutifolia 'Pendulifolia'	3	4	.	.	.	.	.	.	cf	4	yellow

Flower Calendar April—May

— *caprea mas*	3	4	.	.	.	.	cf	zone 4	yellow
— *daphnoides*	3	4	.	.	.	.	cf	4	yellow
— *lucida*	3	4	.	.	.	.	cf	2	yellow
— *aegyptica*	3	4	.	.	.	.	cf	4	yellow
Shepherdia									
argentea	3	4	.	.	.	.	fr	4	yellowish
— *canadensis*	3	4	.	.	.	.	fr	2	yellowish
Acer platanoides	.	4	5	.	.	.	of	3	yellow
— — (red leaved									
types)	.	4	5	.	.	.	of		yellow-red
Cercidiphyllum									
japonicum	.	4	5	.	.	.	of	4	reddish
Cercis									
siliquastrum	.	4	5	.	.	.	of	6	pink
Chamaedaphne									
calyculata	.	4	5	6	.	.	of	3	white
Cornus florida	.	4	5	.	.	.	fr cf of	4	white
Cytisus praecox	.	4	5	.	.	.	of	5	
— — *albus*	.	4	5	.	.	.		cf	white
Daphne cneorum	.	4	5	6	.	.	F #	4	dark pink
Dirca palustris	.	4	5	.	.	.		4	bright yellow
Exochorda									
racemosa	.	4	5	.	.	.	cf	4	white
Forsythia									
intermedia									
(and types)	.	4	5	.	.	.	cf	5	yellow
— *suspensa*	.	4	5	.	.	.	cf wg	5	yellow
Halesia carolina	.	4	5	.	.	.	cf fr	4	white
Lonicera coerulea	.	4	5	.	.	.	fr	6	yellowish
— *purpusii*	2	3	4	.	.	.	cf F	4	yellowish
Magnolia									
loebneri	.	4	.	.	.	.	cf	4	white
— *salicifolia*	.	4	.	.	.	.	cf	5	white
Mahonia									
aquifolium	4	5	.	.	.	.	# fr	5	yellow
— *bealei*	4	5	.	.	.	.	fr #	6	yellow
Osmarea burkwoodii	4	5	. . . .				F #	6	white
Osmaronia									
cerasiformis	4	5	.	.	.	.		7	whitish
Ostrya									
carpinifolia	4	.	.	.	.	.		5	catkins, yellow-brown
Paulownia									
tomentosa	4	5	.	.	.	.		5	violet
Phillyrea									
vilmoriniana	4	5	.	.	.	.	#	6	white
Poncirus									
trifoliata	4	5	.	.	.	.	fr	5	white
Prunus avium									
'Plena'	4	5	.	.	.	.	cf	3	white
— *blireana* and									
'Moseri'	4	.	.	.	.	.	of	5	pink

	4	5	6	7	8	9		zone	
— *cerasifera* (and types)	4	.	.	.	.	.	e fr of zone	4	white
— *incisa*	4	.	.	.	.	.		5	white
— *mandschurica*	4	.	.	.	.	.	fr e	4	white
— *persica* (and types)	4	.	.	.	.	.	e	4	pink, red
— *pumila*	4	5	.	.	.	.		4	white
— *sargentii*	4	5	.	.	.	.	of	4	pink
— *serrulata* (and types)	4	5	.	.	.	.	cf of	5	white, pink
— *spinosa*	4	.	.	.	.	.	of e	4	white
— *tenella*	4	.	.	.	.	.		2	white
— *tomentosa*	4	.	.	.	.	.		2	white-pink
— *triloba*	4	5	.	.	.	.	cf	5	pink
— *yedoensis*	4	.	.	.	.	.		5	white-pink
Pyrus, all	4	.	.	.	.	.	fr		white
Ribes odoratum	4	5	.	.	.	.	F	4	cream
— *gordonianum*	4	5	.	.	.	.	cf	4	bronze-red
Rosmarinus officinalis	4	5	.	.	.	.	F #	6	violet
Rubus spectabilis	4	5	6	.	.	.		5	bright red
Sambucus racemosa	4	5	.	.	.	.	fr	4	yellowish
Skimmia reevesiana 'Rubella'	4	5	6	.	.	.	fr #	7	reddish
Spirea prunifolia	4	5	.	.	.	.	cf	4	white
Spirea thunbergii	4	5	.	.	.	.	cf	4	white
Stachyurus praecox	4	.	.	.	.	.	cf	6	yellow
Ulex europaeus	4	5	.	.	.	9		6	yellow
Viburnum prunifolium	4	5	.	.	.	.	of fr	3	white
Acer psuedo-platanus	.	5	.	.	.	.		5	bright yellow
— *spicatum*	.	5	6	.	.	.	of	2	whitish
Actinidia kolomikta	.	5	6	.	.	.	of fr	4	white
Aesculus carnea	.	5	6	.	.	.	of	3	red
— *hippocastanum* 'Baumannii'	.	5	6	.	.	.	of	3	white
— *pavia*	.	5	6	.	.	.	of	5	red
Akebia quinata	.	5	.	.	.	.	cl fr #	4	violet-brown
Amelanchier (types)	.	5	.	.	.	.	of fr	e	white
Andromeda polifolia	.	5	.	.	.	.	m #	2	pink
Arctostaphylos uva ursi	.	5	6	7	8	.	cr S H #	2	white-pink
Aronia, all	.	5	6	.	.	.	fr		white
Berberis, most types	.	5	6	.	.	.			most yellow
— *gagnepainii*	.	5	6	.	.	.	#	5	bright yellow
— *julianae*	.	5	.	.	.	.	#	5	bright yellow
Buddleia alternifolia	.	5	6	.	.	.	cf	5	lilac

Flower Calendar May—June

Callicarpa, all	.	5	.	.	.	.	fr		lilac		
Caragana											
arborescens	.	5	.	.	.	.	fr	zone 2	yellow		
— pygmaea	.	5	6	.	.	.		2	yellow		
Catalpa ovata	.	5	.	.	.	.	of fr	4	yellow and red		
Clematis alpina	.	5	6	7	.	.	cl	4	blue		
— large flowering types	.	5	6	7	8	9	cl		white, lilac pink, red, blue		
— montana (and types)	.	5	.	.	.	.	cl	5	white, reddish		
Colutea											
arborescens	5	6	7	8	.	.	fr	5	yellow		
— media	5	6	7	8	.	.	fr	6	brown		
Cornus alba	5	6	.	.	.	.	fr	2	white		
— alternifolia	5	6	.	.	.	.		4	white		
— kousa	5	6	.	.	.	.		4	white		
— sanguinea	5	6	.	.	.	.	fr	4	cream		
— stolonifera	5	6	.	.	.	.	fr	2	white		
Coronilla emerus	5	6	7	8	9	10		4	yellow		
Cotoneaster, all	5	6	.	.	.	.	fr		white to pink		
— multiflorus	5	6	7	.	.	.	fr	5	white		
Crataegus, all	5	6	.	.	.	.	fr		most white		
— oxycantha 'Paul's Scarlet'	5	6	.	.	.	.	cf	4	red		
Cytisus decumbens	5	6	.	.	.	.		5	gold-yellow		
— kewensis	5	.	.	.	.	.		6	cream-yellow		
— multiflorus	5	6	.	.	.	.		6	white		
— nigricans	.	6	7	.	.	.		5	deep yellow		
— purpureus	5	6	.	.	.	.		5	purple		
— scoparius (and types)	5	6	.	.	.	.		5	gold, brown, red and other colors		
Daphne burkwoodii	5	6	.	.	.	.		5	pink-white		
Davidia											
involucrata	5	6	.	.	.	.	ss	6	white		
Decaisnea											
fargesii	5	6	.	.	.	.		6	green-yellow		
Deutzia gracilis	5	6	.	.	.	.	cf	4	white		
Dryas octopetala	5	6	7	8	.	.		4	white		
Eleagnus											
commutata	5	6	7	.	.	.	of	4	silvery		
Enkianthus											
campanulatus	5	.	.	.	.	.	of	4	yellow and pink		
— perulatus	5	.	.	.	.	.	of	5	white		
Escallonia (types)	5	6	7	8	.	.			pink-white		
Exochorda											
giraldii	5	.	.	.	.	.	cf	5	white		
Forsythia											
viridissima	5	.	.	.	.	.	ss	5	yellow-green		

Fothergilla										
(types)	5	.	.	.	.		cf H m		white
Genista pilosa	5	6	7	.	.		zone 5		yellow
— *radiata*	5	6	7	.	.			6	yellow
— *sagittalis*	5	6	.	.	.			6	yellow
Halesia monticola	5	.	.	.	.			5	white
Iberis										
sempervirens	5	.	.	.	.		cr #	5	white
Itea virginica	5	6	7	.	.			5	white
Jasminum										
beesianum	5	.	.	.	.		cl F	6	red
Kalmia latifolia	5	6	.	.	.		cf # H	4	pink-white
— *polifolia*	5	6	.	.	.		m # H	4	violet-red
Kerria japonica	5	6	.	.	.		cf	4	bright yellow
— — 'Plena'	5	6	7	8	9		cf		deep yellow
Kolkwitzia										
amabilis	5	6	.	.	.		cf	4	pink-white
Laburnum										
anagyroides	5	6	.	.	.			5	yellow
— *watereri* 'Vossi'	5	6	.	.	.			5	yellow
Ledum										
groenlandicum	5	6	.	.	.		# H f	2	white
Leucothoe										
fontanesiana	5	6	.	.	.		ss sh #	4	white
Liriodendron										
tulipifera	5	6	.	.	.			4	yellow-green
Lonicera										
syringantha	5	6	.	.	.			4	pink-lilac
— *tatarica*										
(and types)	5	6	7	.	.			3	pink, red, white
— *xylosteum*										
'Claveyi'	5	6	.	.	.			4	yellowish
Lycium, all	5	6	7	8	9	.	fr		lilac-red
Magnolia obovata	5	6	.	.	.		of	5	white
— *kobus*	5	6	.	.	.			5	white
— *liliiflora*	5	.	.	.	.			5	white
— — 'Nigra'	5	.	.	.	.				deep purple
— *tripetala*	5	6	.	.	.		of	4	white
— *soulangiana*										
(and types)	5	.	.	.	.			5	pink-white
— — 'Lennei'	5	.	.	.	.				red
									white center
Menziesia pilosa	5	6	.	.	.			4	white or pink
Mespilus										
germanica	5	.	.	.	.		fr e	5	white
Neillia sinensis	5	6	.	.	.			4	reddish
Paeonia										
suffruticosa	5	.	.	.	.			5	white, pink, red, lilac
Parrotiopsis										
jaquemont.	5	.	.	.	.		ss	5	white

Flower Calendar May—June

Potentilla										
fruticosa	5	6	7	8	9	10		zone 2	yellow, orange, white, red
Prunus glandulosa										
'Albiplena'	5	.	.	.	.	.		cf	4	white
— — 'Sinensis'	5	.	.	.	.	.		cf		pink-red
— *laurocerasus*	5	.	.	.	.	.		ss-sh #	6	white
— *mahaleb*	5	.	.	.	.	.			6	white
— *padus*	5	.	.	.	.	.			3	white
— *serotina*	5	6	.	.	.	.			3	white
— *spinosa* 'Plena'	5	.	.	.	.	.			4	white
Pterostyrax										
hispida	5	6	.	.	.	.			5	white
Pyracantha, all	5	.	.	.	.	.		fr #		white
Rhodotypos										
scandens	5	6	.	.	.	.		fr	5	white
Ribes										
sanguineum	5	.	.	.	.	.		cf	5	carmine
Robinia hispida	5	6	7	8	.	.		cr	5	pink
Rubus deliciosus	5	.	.	.	.	.			4	white
— *parviflorus*	5	6	7	.	.	.			4	white
Schizandra										
chinensis	5	6	.	.	.	.		cl	4	reddish
Sorbus aria	5	.	.	.	.	.		of fr	5	white
— *aucuparia*	5	.	.	.	.	.		of fr	5	white
— *intermedia*	5	.	.	.	.	.		of fr	5	white
— *hybrida*	5	.	.	.	.	.		fr	4	white
— *koehniana*	5	6	.	.	.	.		fr	5	white
Spartium junceum	5	6	7	8	9	.			7	bright yellow
Spirea arguta	5	.	.	.	.	.		cf	4	white
— *cinerea*	5	.	.	.	.	.		cf	4	white
— *trichocarpa*	5	6	.	.	.	.		cf	4	white
— *vanhouttei*	5	6	.	.	.	.		cf	4	white
Staphylea										
colchica	5	.	.	.	.	.		cf	6	white
— *pinnata*	5	6	.	.	.	.		cf	6	white
— *trifolia*	5	.	.	.	.	.		cf	4	white
Styrax obassia	5	6	.	.	.	.		cf	5	white
Symplocos										
paniculata	5	6	.	.	.	.		fr	5	white
Syringa, see										
list p. 69	5	6	7	.	.	.		cf	F	white, lilac, blue, red
Tamarix										
parviflora	5	.	.	.	.	.			4	bright pink
Vaccinium										
corymbosum	5	.	.	.	.	.		fr e	3	white
Viburnum										
burkwoodii	5	.	.	.	.	.		cf F	5	white-pink
— *carlcephalum*	5	.	.	.	.	.		cf F	5	white
— *carlesii*	5	.	.	.	.	.		cf F	4	white
— *dentatum*	5	6	.	.	.	.		fr	2	white

— *hupehense*	5	.	.	.	.	.	of fr zone 5		white
— *lantana*	5	6	.	.	.	.	of fr	3	white
— *lentago*	5	6	.	.	.	.	of fr	2	white
— *opulus* (and var.)	5	6	.	.	.	.	of cf	3	white
— *plicatum* (and var.)	5	6	.	.	.	.	of cf	4	white
— *rhytidophyllum*	5	6	.	.	.	.	of fr #	5	white
— *sargentii*	5	6	.	.	.	.	fr	4	white
— *wrightii*	5	6	7	.	.	.	of fr	5	white-pink
— — 'Hessei'	5	6	.	.	.	.	of fr		white
Vinca minor	5	6	7	8	9	.	cr #	4	blue, also violet and white
Weigela (and var.)	5	6	.	.	.	.	cf	5	white, pink, red
Wisteria floribunda	5	6	.	.	.	.	cl F	4	violet
— *sinensis*	5	6	.	.	.	.	cl F	5	violet
Zenobia pulverulenta	5	6	.	.	.	.	F	5	white
Actinidia arguta	.	6	.	.	.	.	fr e F,	4	white
— *polygama*	.	6	.	.	.	.	fr e F	4	white
Aesculus flava	.	6	.	.	.	.		3	yellow
Ailanthus altissima	.	6	7	.	.	.	of	4	green-yellow
Amorpha fruticosa	.	6	.	.	.	.		4	violet
Aristolchia macrophylla	.	6	7	.	.	.	of cl	4	yellow-brown
Bruckenthalia spiculifolia	.	6	7	.	.	.	cr S H	5	pink
Calluna, see list p. 50	.	6	7	8	9	.	cr cf		white, lilac, red
Calycanthus floridus	.	6	7	.	.	.	ss F	4	deep brown
— *fertilis*	.	6	7	.	.	.	ss F	4	bright brown
Castanea sativa	.	6	.	.	.	.	e	5	cream
Catalpa bignonioides	6	.	.	.	.			4	white, dotted
— *speciosa*	6	.	.	.	.			4	as above
Celastrus, all	6	.	.	.	.		cl fr		greenish, not noticeable
Chionanthus virginicus	6	.	.	.	.		fr	4	white
Cornus amomum	6	.	.	.	.			5	white
— *racemosa*	6	7	.	.	.			4	white
Cotinus coggygria	6	7	.	.	.		of fr	5	greenish
— — 'Purpurea'	6	7	.	.	.		of fr		reddish
Daboecia cantabrica	6	.	.	.	.		cr S H	5	purple
Daphne arbuscula	6	.	.	.	.		#	5	pink
Deutzia magnifica	6	.	.	.	.		cf	5	white
— *rosea* (and var.)	6	7	.	.	.		cf	5	white to pink-white
— *scabra* (and var.)	6	7	.	.	.		cf	5	white to reddish
Diervilla, all	6	7	8	.	.		cr sh		bright yellow

Flower Calendar June—July

Species	Months	Code	Zone	Color
Eleagnus				
angustifolia	6	of fr	2	silvery
— umbellata	6	of fr	3	yellowish
Escallonia				
langleyensis	6 7 . . .	cf ss	8	deep pink
Evodia hupehensis	6	of fr F	5	white
Euonymous yedoensis	6	fr	4	yellow-red
Genista hispanica	6 7 . . .	cr	6	yellow
— tinctora	6 7 8 . .	cf	2	yellow
Halimodendron				
halodendron	6 7 . . .	S	2	purple
Hebe spp.	6 7 . . .			white, blue, red
Hydrangea arb.				
'Grandiflora'	6 7 8 9 .	cf	4	white
Indigofera potaninii	6 7 . . .	cf S	5	lilac-pink
Jasminum floridum	6 7 8 . .		8	yellow
— officinale	6 7 8 9 .	F	7	white
— stephanense	6	F	6	pink
Kalmia angustifolia	6 7 . . .	#	2	pink
— — 'Rubra'	6 7 . . .	#		dark red
Ligustrum, all	6 7 . . .			white
Laburnum alpinum	6		4	yellow
Lonicera caprifolium	6 7 . . .	cl fr F	4	yellow-red
— iberica	6		5	cream
— involucrata	6	fr	5	yellow-red
— maackii	6	fr	2	white
— morrowii	6	fr	4	whitish-yellow
Maackia amurensis	6 7 . . .		4	greenish white
Magnolia sieboldii	6 7 . . .		5	white and red
Osmanthus				
heterophyllus	6 7 . . .	F #	6	white
Myricaria germanica	6 7 . . .		6	bright pink
Oxydendrum arboreum	6 7 8 . .	of	5	white
Phellodendron, all	6	fr of F		green-yellow
Philadelphus,				
(and var.)	6 7 . . .			white
Photinia villosa	6	of fr	4	white
Physocarpus, all	6 7 . . .			whitish
Rhododendron				
maximum	6 7 . . .		3	light pink
Rhus typhina	6 7 . . .	fr of	5	red panicle
Robinia holdtii				
britzensis	6 . 8 9 .	S	5	bright pink
— kelseyi	6	S	5	lilac-pink
— psuedoacacia	6	S	3	white
— — 'Semperflorens'	6 7 8 9 .	S		white
— viscosa	6 7 8 . .	S	3	bright pink
Rubus				
cockburnianus	6	ss H	4	reddish
— odoratus	6 7 8 . .	ss sh H	3	purple
Sambucus nigra	6 7 . . .	fr e su-sh		
		u	5	white

Sophora japonica		7	.	.	.	zone	4	cream white
Sorbus vilmorinii	6	.	.	.	.	of ft	5	white
Spirea bumalda								
(and var.)	6	7	.	.	.		5	pink, white
— *decumbens*	6	.	.	.	.		5	white
— *henryi*	6	.	.	.	.	cf	5	white
— *japonica*								
(and var.)	6	7	.	.	.		5	red
— *menziesii*	6	7	8	.	.		6	bright red
— *nipponica*	6	.	.	.	.		4	white
— *trilobata*	6	.	.	.	.	cf	4	white
— *veitchii*	6	7	8	.	.	cf	5	white
— *sargentiana*	6	.	.	.	.	cf	5	white
Stephanandra incisa	6	7	.	.	.		5	whitish
— *tanakae*	6	7	.	.	.		4	yellowish-white
Stranvaesia								
davidiana	6	.	.	.	.	fr ss u #	7	white
Styrax japonica	6	7	.	.	.		5	white
Symphoricarpos albus	6	7	.	.	.	fr ss sh u	3	white
Tamarix pentandra	6	7	.	.	.		2	bright pink
Tilia europaea	6	7	.	.	.	F	3	yellowish
— *platyphylla*	6	.	.	.	.	F	3	yellowish
Viburnum plicatum								
(and var.)	6	.	.	.	.	of cf	4	white
— *pubescens*	6	7	.	.	.	fr	4	white
Xanthorrhiza								
simplicissima	6	7	.	.	.	cr ss	4	yellow-brown
Amorpha canescens	.	7	.	.	.		2	violet-brown
Buddleia								
davidii (and var.)	.	7	8	9	.	cf	5	white, lilac red, blue
Ceanothus americanus	.	7	.	.	.	cf	4	white
Cephalanthus								
occidentalis	.	7	8	9	.		4	white
Campsis radicans	.	7	8	9	.	cl	4	red
Cistus laurifolius	7	8	.	.	.	#	7	white
Clematis vitalba	7	8	9	.	.		4	white
Clethra, all	7	8	9	.	.	ss H	H	white
Cytisus austriacus	7	8	.	.	.	S	5	golden yellow
Fuchsia gracilis	7	8	9	10		ss H	7	red
Hibiscus syriacus								
(and var.)	7	8	9	.	.	cf	5	pink, red blue, white
Holodiscus discolor	7	.	.	.	.	cf	5	white
Hydrangea aspera	7	8	.	.	.	cf	7	light blue
—— *sargentiana*	7	8	.	.	.	of		white-violet
— *paniculata*								
'Grandiflora'	7	8	.	.	.	cf	4	white turning red
— *quercifolia*	7	8	9	.	.	cf of	5	white turning red

Flower Calendar August—September

— macrophylla (and var.)	7	8	.	.	.	of zone 5	white, pink red, blue
Hypericum androsaemum	7	8	9	.	.	fr cf 4	yellow
— moserianum	7	8	9	.	.	7	yellow
— patulum (and var.)	7	8	9	.	.	cf 6	yellow
Indigofera gerardiana	7	8	9	.	.	5	purple
Koelreuteria paniculata	7	8	.	.	.	fr 5	yellow
Laburnocytisus adamii	7	.	.	.	.	5	pink and yellow
Lespedeza bicolor	7	8	9	.	.	4	violet-red
Leycesteria formosa	7	8	9	.	.	fr 7	light violet
Lonicera browni	7	8	.	.	.	cl 5	red
— involucrata 'Serotina'	7	8	.	.	.	5	yellow-red
Periploca gracea	7	8	.	.	.	cl fr 8	brown-violet
Polygonum aubertii	7	8	9	.	.	cl 4	white
Rubus ulmifolius 'Bellidiflorus'	7	8	.	.	.	4	pink
Sambucus canadensis	7	8	.	.	.	su-ss fr 3	white
— — 'Maxima'	7	8	.	.	.	su-ss fr	white
Sorbaria arborea	7	8	.	.	.	5	white
Spirea albiflora	7	8	.	.	.	4	white
— bumalda 'Crispa'	7	8	.	.	.	5	red
— douglasii	7	8	.	.	.	5	purple
Stewartia pseudocamellia	7	8	.	.	.	of 5	white
Symphoricarpos chenaultii	7	.	.	.	.	fr su-ss 4	pink
— orbiculatus	7	.	.	.	.	fr su-ss 2	pink-white
Tilia cordata	7	.	.	.	.	F 3	yellowish
— petiolaris	7	.	.	.	.	F 5	yellowish
— tomentosa	7	8	.	.	.	4	yellowish
Aesculus parviflora	.	8	.	.	.	cr 4	white
Aralia chinensis	.	8	.	.	.	of fr 3	white
— elata	.	8	.	.	.	of fr 3	white
Caryopteris clandonensis	.	8	9	.	.	cf F 5	violet-blue
Clematis heracleifolia	.	8	9	.	.	cf 4	bright blue
— paniculata	.	8	9	.	.	cl cf F 5	white
Clerodendrum trichotomum		8	9	.	.	fr F 6	white-red
Elsholtzia stauntonii	.	.	9	10		F 4	purple
Hamamelis virginiana	.	.	9	10.		H F 4	bright yellow
Hypericum calycinum	.	8	9	.	.	su-sh cr H	yellow
						# 6	

38

Species	8	9	10	11	12	1	2	3	4	code	zone	color
Perovskia												
abrotanoides	8	.	.	.						of F	4	bright blue
— *atriplicifolia*	8	9	10	.						of F	4	violet
Sophora japonica	8	.	.	.							4	cream white
Tilia euchlora	8	.	.	.						of F	5	yellowish
Yucca filamentosa	8	9	.	.						of	4	white
Jasminum nudiflorum	.	.	11	12	1	2	3			cl cf	5	yellow
Hamamelis japonica	.	.	.	.	1	2	3			cf H	4	yellow
—— *zuccariniana*	.	.	.	.	1	2	3			cf H		bright yellow
—— *flavo-purpur-escens*	.	.	.	.	1	2	3			cf H		reddish
Hamamelis mollis	.	.	.	.	1	2	3			cf H	5	deep yellow
—— 'Brevipetala'	.	.	.	.	1	2	3			cf|H		orange
— *vernalis*	.	.	.	.	1	2	.			H	4	green-yellow
Salix daphnoides 'Praecox'	(9	10	11	12)	1	2	3			cf	4	yellow
— *acutifolia* 'Pendulifolia'	.	.	.	.	1	2	3			cf	4	yellow
Acer saccharinum	.	.	.	.	.	2	3				3	bright yellow
Betula, **all**	.	.	.	.	.	2	3	4		of cf		yellow
Corylus, **all**	.	.	.	.	.	2	3			cf e		yellow
Viburnum bodnantense	.	10	11	12	1	2	3			F	6	pink-white
— *farreri* (=fragrans)	.	.	12	1	2	3	4			F	5	clear pink
Chimonanthus praecox	.	.	.	.	.	2	3	.		F	7	light yellow

Heath & Heather

d. Flowering Calendar and List; Erica and Calluna

all # su-ss cr

Name	Zone	Flowering months	Code	Color
Erica carnea, red	zone 5			
'Vivelli'		12 1 2 3	A	
'Ruby Glow'		3 4	A	
'Praecox Rubra'		3 4	A	
Erica carnea, pink				
'Winter Beauty'		12 1 2 3	A	
'Springwood Pink'		1 2 3	A	
'James Backhouse'		3 4	A	
Erica carnea, white				
'Springwood'		1 2 3	A	
Erica mediterranea	7			
'Brightness'		3 4 5	A	red
'Coccinea'		3 4 5	A	red
'Silberschmelze'		3 4 5	A	white
Erica cinerea,	5			
'Coccinea'	5	6 7 8	H	red
'Alba'		6 7	H	white
'Rosea'		6 7	H	pink
'C.G. Best'		7 8 9	H	salmon-pink
'Atrosanguinea'		7 8	H	red
'C.D. Eason'		7 8	H	pink
'Pallas'		7 8 9	H	lilac
Erica tetralix, zone 3				
'Con. Underwood'		6 7 8 9 10	H	red
'Alba Mollis'		7 8 9	H	white
'Ken. Underwood'		7 8 9	H	pink
'Alba'		7 8 9	H	white
Erica vagans,	5			
'Lyonesse'		8 9 10	A-H	white
'Mrs. D.F. Maxwell'		8 9 10	A-H	white
'St. Keverne'		8 9 10	A-H	salmon
Calluna vulgaris, zone 4				
'Tib'		7 8 9	S H	red
'Tenuis'		7 8 9 10	S H	red
'County Wicklow'		8 9	S H	pink
C.W. Nix'		8 9	S H	red
'Mairs Variety'		8 9	S H	white
'Mullion'		8 9	S H	pink
'Roma'		8 9	S H	red
'Alba Plena'		8 9 10	S H	white
'Alporti'		8 9 10	S H	red
'H.E. Beale'		8 9 10	S H	pink
'J.H. Hamilton'		8 9	S H	pink
'Elegantissima'		9 10	S H	white
'Goldsworth Crimson'		9 10	S H	red
'David Eason'		10 11	S H	red

COMPANION PLANTS FOR ERICA AND CALLUNA

Groundcovers

Juniperus, creeping types # of
Andromeda polifolia zone 2 # fl
Arctostaphylos uva-ursi 2 # of
Cassiope tetragona 7 # of fl
Cotoneaster dammeri 5 # of
Daboecia cantabrica 5 # fl

Dryas octopetala 4 # of fl fr
Empetrum nigrum 2 # of
Epigea repens 2 # fl F
Hypericum coris 6 fl
Phyllodoce coerulea 2 # fl
Vaccinium oxycoccos 2 # fr
Thymus serpyllum 4 of fl

Plants as Tall as Erica and Calluna

Berberis, low growing types
Cotoneaster conspicuus
    'Decorus' zone 6 of fl
— *congestus* 6 # of fl
— *horizontalis,* types 4 of fr
— *praecox* 4 of fl fr
— *Daphne cneorum* 4 # of fl
Genista hispanica 6 fl
— *lydia* 7 fl
— *sagittalis* 6 fl
Hebe armstrongii 7 # of

Hebe cupressoides 7 # of
— *hectori* 7 # of

Itea virginica 5 fl F
Kalmiopsis leachiana 6 # fl
Ledum groenlandicum 2 # of fl
Lithospermum diffusum 6 fl
Lonicera pileata 5 # of
Loiseleuria procumbens 2 # of fl
Moltkia petraea 6 fl
Teucrium chamaedrys 5 # of fl
Ulex europaeus 6 fl

Flower Calendar Rhododendron

flowering time	violet to bluish	lilac to reddish	red
April	Ramapo	PJM Purple Gem	Nobleanum Unknown Warrior
early May	Blue Peter Old Port Susan	Giganteum Progress	Scarlet Wonder C.B. van Ness Cynthia Hassan Max Sye

mid May	Leopold
	Purple
	  Splendor
	Purpureum
	  Grandiflorum
		Alfred
		Bibber
		catawbiense
		  Boursault
		  Grandiflorum
		Charles Dickens
		Dr. H.C. Dresselhuys
		E.S. Rand
		Everestianum
		Mexico
		Raphael
		Roseum Elegans
			America
			Britannia
			Dr. V.H. Rutgers
			F.D. Godman
			Hugh Koster
			Omega
			Mrs. P. den Ouden
			Trilby
			William Austin
			Carmen
			Gen. Eisenhower

late May	Lees Dark
	  Purple
	Purpureum
	  Elegans
	Blue Ensign
	Marchioness of
	  Lansdowne
		Allah
		Caractacus
		Dietrich
		Holger
		Humboldt
		Oldewig
		Parsons
		  Gloriosum
		Roseum
		  Superbum
			James Marshall
			  Brooks
			Louis Pasteur
			van den Broeke
			van der Hoop
			Vulcan
			John Walter
			Kluis Sensation
			Lord Roberts
			Nova Zembla

June	Black Beauty Blue Jay		Moser's Maroon Red Cap

Rhododendron and Azaleas

RHODODENDRON HYBRIDS

pink	white or light shades	yellow	flowering time
Christmas Cheer Cleopatra Prince Camille de Rohan	Boule de neige Jacksonii Rosamundi	Cunninghams Sulfur Canary Diane	April
Countess of Athlone Mrs. C.B. van Ness Mrs. G.W. Leak N.N. Sherwood	Bismark Beauty of Littleworth Jewess	Adriaan Koster Goldsworth Yellow Zuiderzee Harvest Moon Kosters Cream Unique	early May
Catherine van Tol Director E. Hjelm Homer Mrs. R.S. Holford Pink Pearl Prof. Hugo de Vries Marinus Koster	Album Novum Eidam Genoveva Gudrun Hero Leopardi Mrs. Lindsay Smith Cunninghams White		mid May
Antoon van Welie Kate Waterer Lady Annette de Trafford Clementine Lemaire Duke of York Scintillation English Roseum	catawbiense Album Gomer Waterer Mme. Carvalho Mme. Masson Delicatessimum Sappho Chinoides		late May
Edith Alice Martineau	Polar Bear		June

Azaleas

A. "Mollis" types
(deciduous) zone 5
yellow to orange-yellow
'Adriaan Koster', best pure yellow type
'Sunburst', dark yellow, larger blooming
'Director Moerlands', dark yellow
'Christopher Wren', orange-yellow, large flower cluster
'Hortulanus H. Witte', bright orange-yellow
orange-yellow to salmon orange
'Salmon Queen', apricot yellow with salmon pink
'Lemnora', apricot yellow with pink-orange spot
'Frans van der Bom', salmon orange
'Hugo Koster', dark salmon orange
'Koningin Emma', dark orange with salmon
orange to orange-red
'Polly Claessens', pure orange, large flowering
'Winston Churchill', orange with red
'Orange Glow', orange with red
'Dr. M. Oosthoek', dark orange-red
'Koster's Brilliant Red', orange-red (not the best in its color)
'Speks Brilliant', orange-red
red
'Willem Hardijzer', dark red with some orange
'Catharina Rinke', red with orange, dark markings, large flowers, late
'Radiant', best dark red type
pink
'Suzanne Loef', dark pink-red

B. Ghent Hybrids
(deciduous) zone 4
yellow
'Nancy Waterer', gold yellow
'Narcissiflora', sulfur yellow, full
pink
'Corneille', soft pink, rosette form, full
'Bouquet de Flore', bright pink with white and yellow
'Fanny' (= 'Pucella'), dark purple-pink, very early
red
'Sang de Gentbrugge', bright red, longer blooming than 'Satan'
'Pallas', geranium red, orange spot, early
orange
'Coccinea Speciosa', light orange, abundant
white
'Daviesii', cream white, yellow spots, blue-green foliage

C. Rustica Hybrids, all full, compact growing
(deciduous) zone 4
'Aida', soft pink with lilac tone, full
'Freya', salmon with yellow cast, full

'Norma', pink with salmon, full
'Phebe', sulfur yellow, full
'Velasquez', cream white with soft pink tints, full

D. 'Knap Hill' and 'Exbury' Hybrids
(deciduous hybrids bred for larger flowers and better color) zone 5
'Ballerina', white, small yellow spots, very large flower
'Balzac', dark orange-red, fringe wavy
'Basilisk', bright yellow, spotted, large flower
'Berryrose', pink, large yellow spots, large bloom
'Cecile', dark pink, yellow spotted, large bloom
'Fireball', dark red
'Gallipoli,' carmin-pink, large blooms, open
'Gibraltar', deep orange, petals fringed
'Gold Dust', gold-yellow with orange, large bloom
'Golden Eagle', strong orange
'Golden Sunset', deep yellow, orange spot, very large
'Hotspur Orange', deep orange, large flower
'Hotspur Red', flame red
'Klondyke', deep golden yellow, large open bloom
'Persil', white, spotted yellow
'Royal Command', vermillion
'Satan', dark geranium red, blooms smaller
'Strawberry Ice', bright pink with orange, large
'Sylphides', bright pink, large flower
'Toucon', cream yellow, yellow spots, very early, large

E. 'Japanese' Azaleas
(evergreen) zone 6
'Addy Wery', dark vermillion, small bloom, early
'Aladdin', bright geranium red, small, early
'Apple Blossom', pale pink with white throat
'Beethoven', lilac, large midseason
'Betty', medium pink, midseason
'Blaauws Pink', salmon pink, early
'Campfire' (= 'Hino-scarlet'), deep red, small, early
'Christina', carmin, full, very large, mid-early
'Christmas Cheer', bright red, hose-in-hose
'Coral Bells', clear pink, hose-in-hose, midsedason
'Delaware Valley White', white single, late, hardy
'Favorite', deep pink, hardy, early
'Fedora', deep pink, large, hardy, midseason
'Hersey Red', red, hose-in-hose, midseason
'Hino-crimson', red, single, midseason
'Hinodegiri', red, single, midseason
'Kathleen', dark pink, large, very hardy
'Lilac Time', dark lilac, large, mid-early
'Mother's Day', deep carmine red, double flower
'Multiflora', lilac, very small bloom, very hardy
'Orange Beauty', orange, wide plant, very hardy
'Palestrina', white, green middle, very hardy
'Purple Splendor', violet, large bloom, very hardy

Rhododendron Species

'Rosebud', rose pink, hose-in-hose, late
'Snow', white, hose-in-hose, midseason
'Stewartstonian', red, single, late, very hardy
'Tradition', pink, hose-in-hose, midseason, hardy
'Vuyk's Scarlet', deep red, large, midseason

F. Repens Hybrids
(low growing evergreen types from D. Hobbie, height 50—70 cm., width ove 1m) zone 5
'Abendglut', deep red, May
'Aksel Olsen', blood red, mid May
'Baden-Baden', scarlet, May
'Bad Eilsen', scarlet, early May
'Bengal', scarlet, May
'Elisabeth Hobbie', dark scarlet-red
'Juwel', dark scarlet red, May
'Red Carpet', light red, late April
'Salute', dark blood red, May
'Scarlet Wonder', scarlet, May

RHODODENDRON SPECIES

Dwarf types, under 50cm
Evergreen
Rh. calostrotum, zone 4, violet, April 30 cm
Rh. fastigiatum, 5 purple, April-May, 50 cm
Rh. impeditum, 4 violet, April, dense cushion form, 30-50 cm
Rh. keleticum, 4 purple-violet, April, 5 cm
Rh. radicans, 4 purple-violet, May, 5—10cm

Deciduous
Rh. camtschaticum, 3 purple-violet, June—Sept. 10 cm

Low growing, 50—100 cm
Evergreen
Rh. caucasicum, 4 pink, May, 100 cm
Rh. chryseum, 4 yellow, April—May, 20—70 cm
Rh. ferrugineum, 4 pink, May, 60—80 cm
Rh. haematodes, 5 dark red, May, 60—80 cm
Rh. hippophaeoides, 5 lilac, April, 50 cm
Rh. hirsutum, 4 pink, June, 60—80 cm
Rh. impeditum 'Blue Diamond', 4 blue, May, 60 cm
Rh. impeditum 'Blue Tit', 4 violet-blue, April—May, 50—100 cm
Rh. laetevirens, 4 pink, May 60—80 cm
Rh. trichostomum, 6 pink, May, 50 cm
Rh. micranthum, 4 white, July, 100 cm
Rh. obtusum, 6 pink to red, May, 50—100 cm, semi-deciduous
Rh. racemosum, 5 pink, April, 60-100 cm
Rh. russatum, 5 violet, April—May, 50—80 cm

Rh. williamsianum, 5 pink, April, 50—100 cm

Deciduous
Rh. canadense, 3 lilac, April, 30-60 cm

Medium height, 100—200 cm
Evergreen
Rh. ambiguum, 5 yellow with green, April—May, 100—150 cm
Rh. augustinii, 7 lavender-blue, May, 150—200 cm
Rh. campylocarpum, 6 yellow, April—May 100—200 cm
Rh. carolinianum, 4 pink, May—June, 100-150 cm
Rh. degronianum, 6 pink, May—June, 100—150 cm
Rh. makinoi, 6 pink, June, 100—200 cm
Rh. metternichi, 4 pink, April, 100—200 cm
Rh. orbiculare, 5 pink-red, April, 100—150 cm
Rh. oreodoxa, 5 pink, March-April, 150—200 cm
Rh. oreotrephes, 4 lilac, April—May, 100—200 cm
Rh. ponticum 'Imbricatum, 5 violet, June, 100—150 cm
Rh. wardii, 6 yellow, May, 100—200 cm
Rh. wightii, 5 yellow, April, 100-150 cm
Rh. williamsianum (Hobbie hybrids), 5 pink-red, April—May, 100—150 cm
Rh. yunnanense, 4 bright red, May, 100—200 cm

Deciduous
Rh. albrechtii, 5 pink, April—May
Rh. japonicum (=Azalea mollis), 4 orange to red, May, 100—200 cm
Rh. occidentale, 6 white, June, 100—150 cm
Rh. quinquefolium, 4 pink-white, March—April, 100—150 cm
Rh. reticulatum, 4 lilac, April—May, 100—200 cm
Rh. vaseyi, 4 bright pink, April, 100—200 cm
Rh. viscosum, 3 white, July, 100-150 cm

Height, over 100 cm
Evergreen
Rh. argyrophyllum, 5 pink-red, April, 200—300 cm
Rh. brachycarpum, 6 white-pink, June—July, 200—300 cm
Rh. campanulatum, 5 pink to white, April—May, 200 cm+
Rh. decorum, 5 birght pink, March—June, 200 cm
Rh. fortunei, 6 pink-white, May, fragrant, 200—300 cm
Rh. ponticum,. 5 purple-violet, June, 200—500 cm
Rh. ponticum 'Roseum', 5 bright pink, June—July, 200—300 cm
Rh. smirnowii, 4 pink, June, 100—300 cm
Rh. sutchuenense, 5 pink, March—April, 200—300 cm

Deciduous
Rh. luteum (=Azalea pontica), 5 yellow, fragrant, May, 100—400 cm
Rh. schlippenbachii, 4 bright pink, April—May, 200—250 cm

Crabapple List

f. Crabapple List (*Malus*)

(in order of bloom, all disease resistant types)

baccata mandschurica		zone 2	white, simple, very early, blooms every year, red fruit
baccata	of	4	white, early, blooms yearly, fruit red to yellow
'Flame'		2	white, early, rounded tree, fruit small, bright yellow
'Bob White'	F	4	white, early, rounded dense, fruit small, yellow
'Liset'	of	4	purple, simple, early, bronze fall foliage
'Indian Magic'		4	rose red, early, semi upright, fruit glossy red persist all winter
'Makamik'		4	purple, early, blooms yearly, red fruit
'Profusion'	of	4	purple, simple, mid-season, semi-upright, small red fruit
purpurea 'Lemoinei'	of	4	purple-pink, somewhat full, yearly, dense, small red fruit
'Red Jade'		4	white, simple, early, weeping habit, fruit small red, abundant
silvestris 'Plena'		5	white, full, early, bushy , fruit orange, edible
atrosanguinea		4	dark pink, mid-season, fruit yellow
floribunda		4	light pink, mid-season, showy, dense, fruit red and yellow
'Georgeous'		4	pink-white, simple, mid-season, fruit light red
'Royalty'	of	4	crimson, simple, abundant, purple foliage effective all summer, outstanding
'Katherine'		4	bright pink, full, mid-season, blooms biennially, fruit yellow
purpurea 'Aldenhamensis'	of	4	purple, midseason, simple or semi-double, open habit
'Snowcloud'		4	white, double, very attractive in flower, vase shape
spectabilis 'Riversii'		4	pink, full, midseason, fruit yellow
'Van Eseltine'		4	dark pink, full or double flowering, columnar, growth habit
zumi 'Calocarpa'	of	5	light pink, mid-season, biennial, orange fruit
tschonoskii		5	white, mid, tall conical habit, good fall foliage
sargentii		4	white, simple, late, low form, bushy, 2m, fruit small red
sieboldii		5	pink-white, late, fruit yellow
— 'Wintergold'		5	pink-white, simple, late, fruit abundant, yellow
ionensis 'Klehms' Bechtol'	F	2	pink, large and full, grows large and open, fruit scarce

| 'Prince Georges' | of | 5 | pink, double, very late, fruitless |
| *toringoides* 'Macrocarpa' | | 5 | white, very late, biennial, fruit, plentiful, persistant, yellow and red |

g. Rose List

POLYANTHA AND FLORIBUNDA HYBRIDS, ALSO MINIATURE ROSES

(in order of flower color and average height)

Miniature Roses (=Bengal Roses)

'Bit O'Sunshine'	yellow	30 cm
'Scarlet Gem'	scarlet	30 cm
'Red Imp'	crimson	30 cm
'Bo Peep'	shell pink, dbl.	30 cm
'Baby Masquerade'	yellow and red	35 cm
'Gold Coin'	yellow	35 cm
'Starina'	cherry red	35 cm
'Chipper'	coral pink	35 cm
'Cinderella'	white	35 cm

Polyantha Hybrids and Floribunda Roses

Red

'Marlena'	dark red, half full	35 cm
'Meteor'	scarlet, full	35 cm
'Orange Sensation'	orange-red, half	50 cm
'Ruth Leuwerik'	rust red, half full	50 cm
'Coup de Foudre'	fire red, full	50 cm
'Holstein'	dark red, simple	50 cm
'Chatter'	carmine, full	50 cm
'Ambassador'	red-orange, full F	60 cm
'Sundowner'	apricot, full	60 cm
'Orange Triumph'	scarlet, full	60 cm
'Korona'	scarlet, full	60 cm
'Euopeana'	blood red, full	60 cm
'Marina'	orange-red, full	60 cm
'Lilli Marleen'	fire red, full	60 cm
'Fanal'	blood red, half	70 cm
'Olala'	blood red, half	70 cm
'Ama'	blood red, full	70 cm
'Paprika'	brick red, simple	70 cm
'Shreveport'	orange-salmon, half	90—100 cm

Pink

'Tip Top'	clear pink, half	40 cm
'First Edition'	coral pink	50 cm
'Summertime'	bright pink, full F	50 cm
'Junior Miss'	pink, full	60 cm
'Elysium'	salmon pink, full F	60 cm
'Queen Elizabeth'	pink	70 cm

Rose List

'Fashion'	pink, full F	80 cm
'Betty Prior'	salmon pink	80 cm
'Cherish'	salmon pink	120 cm

Yellow
'Allgold'	gold-yellow, full	50 cm
'Goldmarie'	gold-yellow, full	50 cm
'Safari'	bright yellow, full	50 cm
'Gold Badge'	deep yellow, full	60 cm
'Goldilocks'	bright yellow, full	60 cm

Bicolor Types
'Circus'	yellow and red, half full	50 cm
'Rumba'	yellow and red, full	60 cm
'Charleston'	yellow and red, full	70 cm
'Masquerade'	yellow and red, full	70 cm
'Double Delight'	red, yellow and white, half full F	80 cm

White
'Ivory Fashion'	white, half full F	50 cm
'French Lace'	white, full	50 cm
'Sea Foam'	pure white, full	60 cm

BETTER GARDEN ROSES
(most are Hybrid Teas denoted: HT, all full,
ordered by color, F = fragrant, with ! = extra strong)

Red
'Bing Crosby'	orange-red, F	80 cm
'Bob Hope'	bright red, F	90 cm
'Crimson Glory'	deep carmine, F!	50 cm
'Chrysler Imperial'	dark red, F!	60 cm
'Erotica'	dark red, F!	60 cm
'Fragrant Cloud'	coral, F!	70 cm
'Gypsy'	orange-red, F	100 cm
'Mirandy'	wine red, F	60 cm
'Mon Cheri'	pink-red	80 cm
'Mr. Lincoln'	bright red, F	90 cm
'New Yorker'	dark red, F	60 cm
'Super Star'	salmon orange, F	100 cm
'Tradition'	dark red	70 cm

Pink
'Ballet'	pink	70 cm
'First Lady'	pink, F!	60 cm
'First Prize'	bright pink, F	60 cm
'Friendship'	coral pink	90 cm
'Miss All American Beauty'	rich pink	70 cm
'Perfume Delight'	medium pink, F!	70 cm
'Pink Peace'	carmine pink, F!	90 cm

Yellow
'Apollo'	lemon yellow	90 cm
'King's Ransome'	gold-yellow, F	70 cm
'Oregold'	deep yellow, F	70 cm
'Peace'	bright yellow, F	70 cm
'Peer Gynt'	gold yellow, F!	70 cm
'Sutter's Gold'	gold yellow, F!	90 cm

Blue
'Blue Girl'	lavender	80 cm
'Paradise'	lavender	90 cm
'Silver Star'	silver-blue, F!	70 cm

BETTER ROSES FOR CUTTING AND ARRANGING
(HT = Hybrid Tea, FL = Floribunda, SH = Shrub Rose)

Red
'Crimson Glory'	HT dark red, F	50 cm
'Henkell Royal'	HT blood red, F	60 cm
'Lilli Marleen'	FL fire red	60 cm
'Super Star'	HT salmon orange F	100 cm
'Tradition'	HT dark red	70 cm

Pink
'Dana'	HT clear pink, F	80 cm
'First Lady'	HT soft pink, F	60 cm
'Junior Miss'	FL bright pink	60 cm
'Queen Elizabeth'	FL bright pink	80 cm
'Tiffany'	HT salmon pink	70 cm

Yellow
'Brandy'	HT gold orange	90 cm
'Gloria Dei'	HT bright yellow, F	80 cm
'King's Ransom'	HT gold yellow, F	70 cm
'PeerGynt'	HT gold yellow, F	70 cm
'Sutter's Gold'	HT gold yellow, F	90 cm

Bicolor
| 'Kordes Perfecta' | HT pink and yellow, F | 60 cm |
| 'Suspense' | HT scarlet and yellow | 80 cm |

Blue
'Blue Girl'	HT lavender	80 cm
'Paradise'	HT lavender	90 cm
'Silver Star'	HT silvery-blue, F	70 cm

White
'Pascali'	HT pure white	50 cm
'Virgo'	HT pure white	60 cm
'White Knight'	HT pure white	100 cm

Rose List

CLIMBING ROSES

(also appropriate as weeping roses when grafted on a standard, lx = one blooming perod, xx = several blooming periods)

Red

'Blaze Superior'	scarlet-red, half full		2.5—3 m
'Chevy Chase'	deep red, full	xx	3-4 m
'Don Juan'	blood red, full	xx	3 m
'Paul's Scarlet'	scarlet red, full	lx	4—5 m
'Red Fountain'	blood red, full	xx	3 m
'Solo'	dark red, full	xx	2—3 m
'Sympathie'	dark red, full	xx	3-4 m
'Wilhelm Hansmann'	blackish red, half full	xx	3—4 m

Pink

'America'	salmon pink, full	xx	4-5 m
'American Pillar'	rose red, simple	lx	4-5 m
'Chaplin's Pink Climber'	dark pink, half	xx	4—5 m
'Coral Dawn'	coral pink, full	xx	3 m
'New Dawn'	soft pink-white, full	xx	4—5 m
'Rhonda'	medium pink, half	lx	3—4 m

Yellow

'Climbing Peace'	cream gold, full	xx	3—4 m
'Golden Glow'	gold yellow, full	lx	3—4 m
'Golden Showers'	lemon yellow, half	xx	2—3 m
'Joseph's Coat'	red and yellow	xx	2—3 m
'Le Reve'	gold yellow, half	lx	3—4 m
'Reveil Dijonnais'	yellow with red	lx	3—4 m

BELOVED OLD ROSES

(only a small list is presented as these roses may be difficult to find in cultivation)

	Class.	Year	Color	F	Height
Captain Hayward'	H. Perpetual	1893	crimson	F	200 cm
centifolia 'Muscosa'	centif.	1727	dark pink	F	150
cen. 'Muscosa Alba'	centif.	?	white	F	150
'Eugene Furst'	H. Perpetual	1875	crimson	F!	150
'Fisher Holmes'	H. Perpetual	1865	dark red	F!	200
'Frau Karl Druschki'	H. Perpetual	1901	white		100
'Freiburg II'	HT	1917	pink	F!	60
'General Jacqueminot'	H. Perpetual	1852	purple	F!!	150
'Gloire de Chedane-Guinoisseau'	H. Perpetual	1908	rust red	F!	150
'Hermosa'	Bengal	1840	pink	F	80
'Hugh Dickson'	H. Perpetual	1905	crimson	F!	150

'Kaiserin Auguste Victoria'	HT	1891	cream	F!	60	
'La France'	HT	1867	silver-pink	F!	60 cm	
'Marechal Niel'	Tearose	1864	yellow	F!!	200	
'Mme. Caroline Testout'	HT	1890	pink		80	
'Mme. Jules Bouche'	HT	1910	white	F	60	
'Mrs. John Laing'	H. Perpetual	1887	pink	F	150	
'Nuits de Young'	Moss	1845	purple/brown	F	150	
'Ophelia'	HT	1912	salmon/pink	F	60	
'Paul Neyron'	H. Perpetual	1896	pink	F!	200	
'Souvenir de la Malmaison'	Bourb.	1843	pink		300	
'Ulrich Brunner'	H. Perpetual	1882	bright red	F!	200	

SHRUB AND PARK ROSES

(large, floriferous bush form roses for use in larger gardens and parks, ordered by color and height)

	Color	Flower		
Height 250—300 cm				
'Parkfeuer'	light red	simple	lx	
'Dortmund'	red, white-center	simple	xx	
'Conrad Ferd. Meyer'	pink	full	xx	F!
'Spring Gold'	bright yellow	simple	lx	F
Height to 200 cm				
'Canina von Kiese'	blood red	simple	lx	
'Park Jewel'	rust red	full	lx	F!
'Bonn'	bright red	full	xx	F
'Wilhelm'	red	full	xx	
'Ruskin'	dark red	full	xx	F!
'Hansa'	violet-carmine	full	xx	F!
'Spring Morning'	carmine-pink	simple	lx	
'Fritz Nobis'	yellowish pink	full	lx	F!
'Elmshorn'	salmon pink	full	xx	
'Mozart'	pink	simple	xx	F!
'May Gold'	yelow	full	lx	F!
'Gold Bush'	gold-yellow	full	lx	
'Nevada'	white	simple	lx	
Height to 150 cm				
'Wilhelm Hansmann'	deep red	half full	xx	F
'Prestige'	fire red	half full	xx	
'Berlin'	red	simple	xx	
'Fireworks'	orange	half full	xx	
'Friedrich Heyer'	bright red	simple	xx	
'Claus Groth'	salmon pink	half full	lx	F
'Kathleen Ferrier'	pink	half full	xx	
'Bayreuth'	yellow-red	half full	xx	F

Rose List

'Snow Witch'	white	full	xx	
'Blanc Double de Coubert'	white	full	xx	F!!

Height to 100 cm

'F.J. Grootendorst'	carmine-red	full	xx	
'Andersonii'	carmine-pink	simple	lx	
'Lyric'	pink	simple	xx	
'Pink Grootendorst'	pink	full	xx	
'Grandmaster'	orange-yellow	half full	xx	F
'Plomin'	soft yellow-pink	half full	xx	
'Blance Moreau'	white	full	xx	F!
'Spring Snow'	white	half full	xx	
'Snow Umbrella'	white	simple	xx	

ROSES THORNLESS (and nearly so)

Rosa acicularis, zone 4, pink, simple, 1 m high
— *blanda,* 2, pink, simple, 2 m high
— *banksiae* (and var.), 7, full white or bright yellow, 3 m
— *majalis* (=cinnamomea), 5, carmine, simple, 1.5 m
— *multiflora* (thornless form), 5, white, simple, 3m
— *pendulina* (=alpina), 5, pink, simple, 1 m
— *lheritieranea* (Boursault-Rose), 4, pink, full, very large, 4 m
— 'Amadis', climber, deep purple, full, 4 m
— 'Maria Lisa', climber, pink, white center, small, simple, 3 m
— 'Mme. Sancy de Parabere', climber, pink, large, half full, 4 m
— 'Tausendschon', climber, pink, very full, small, 3 m

SPECIES ROSES
(including some varieties, ordered by size)

Height 200—400 cm

R. haematodes	zone 5	red	250 cm
R. hugonis	5	yellow	200—250 cm
R. multiflora	5	white	300 cm
R. moyesii	5	red	250 cm
R. multibracteata	5	pink	200 cm
R. sericea pteracantha	5	white	300 cm
R. rubiginosa	5	pink-white	300 cm
R. rubrifolia	2	carmine-pink	400 cm
R. setigera	4	pink	300 cm
R. sweginzowii 'Macrocarpa'	4	red	200 cm
R. willmottiae	5	carmine-pink	250 cm

Height 100-200 cm

R. alba 'Suaveolens'	4	white, full	200 cm
R. foetida 'Bicolor Atropurpurea'	4	yellow-red	150 cm
R. gallica 'Splendens'	5	red	150-200 cm

R. roxburghii	5	off white	200 cm
R. rugosa	2	red, pink, white	100—150 cm
R. setipoda	5	pink	200 cm
R. spinosissima		pink-white	120 cm
R. villosa	6	pink	150 cm
R. virginiana	3	pink	120 cm
R. xanthina	5	yellow	150 cm

Height 50—100 cm

R. nitida	3	pink	60—80 cm
R. paulii	5	white	prostrate
R. 'Persian Yellow'	5	yellow	100 cm
R. spinosissima 'Altaica'	4	white	100 cm

ROSES AS GROUNDCOVER

(When planted on weed free slopes these roses will quickly dominate the area. Not recommended for small gardens.)

Rosa wichuriana, zone 5	1 per 3m²	30 cm	white	strong grower
R. 'Max Graf', 5	1 per 1m²	50—60	pink-white	strong grower
R. paulii, 5 (repens alba)	1 per 3m²	60	white	wide branching
R. nitida, 3	6 per 1m²	60—80	pink	stays low
R. virginiana, 3	1 per 1m²	100	pink	strong grower
R. 'The Fairy', 5	2 per 1m²	60	pink	very dense
R. spinosissima, 4	5 per 1m²	50	yellow	likes sand

h. Lilacs

A selection of the better Lilacs (Syringa vulgaris) (hybrids) with international merit. All zone 3

Flowers white

single
'Jan van Tol'
'Marie Legraye'
'Mme. Florent Stepman'
'Vestale'

double
'Alice Harding'
'Mme. Lemoine'
'Monique Lemoine'
'Mme. Casimir Perier'

Flowers yellow, single
'Primrose'

Flowers red to violet-red

single
'Andenken an L. Spath'
'Charles X'
'Reamur'
'Ruhm von Horstenstein'

double
'Charles Joly'
'Mme. Edward Harding'
'Paul Thirion'

Fragrant Plants

Flowers pink to lilac

single
'Catinat'
'Christopher Columbus'
'Lucie Baltet'
'Macrostachya'
'Marechal Foch'

double
'Katherine Havemeyer'
'Leon Gambetta'
'Michel Buchner'
'Mme. Antoine Buchner'
'Oliver de Serres'
'Paul Deschanel'

Flowers lilac-blue

single
'Alphonse Lavalle'
'Clarkes Giant'
'Decaisne'

double
'Duc de Massa'
'President Grevy'

4. Plants with Aromatic Flowers or Foliage

(with flower color and months of bloom)

Abelia grandiflora, 3, foliage pungent when crushed
— *concolor*, 4, as above
Actinidia spp., fragrant flowers
Akebia quinata, 4, flowers purple, 4-5, strong fragrange, fr
Arbutus menziesii, 7, flowers fragrant in May
Artemesia spp., foliage aromatic, grey green
Azara spp., flowers vanilla scented, early spring
Buddleia davidii (and var.), 5, lilac to violet, red and white 7—8, fl
Buxus sempervirens, 5, # foliage scented, sweet scent in flower
Calycanthus floridus, 4, flowers and foliage very aromatic, 7—10
Carissa grandiflora, 9, flowers white, fragrant
Carpenteria californica, 8, white flowers, summer
Caryopteris clandonensis, 7, flowers blue 8—10, foliage scented
— *incana*, 5, blue 8—10, foliage scented
Cedrus spp., foliage aromatic when crushed
Cercidiphyllum japonicum, 4, autumn foliage smells of gingerbread
Chimonanthus praecox, 7, blooms bright yellow, 2—3
Chionanthus virginica, 4, blooms white, slight fragrance, 6
Choisya ternata, 7, white flowers sweet smelling, 5 # foliage also scented
Citrus spp. flowers fragrant
Cladrastus lutea, 3, pendulous white flowers, fragrant, 6
Clematis flammula, 6, white, 7—10, almond scented
Clematis rehderiana, zone 4, yellow, bell shaped, 9—10, fl
— *vitalba*, 4, white, 7—9, almond scented, fr
Clerodendrum trichotomum, 6, white flowers fragrant, August, foliage also aromatic
— — *fargesii*, 6, as above, fr
Clethra alnifolia, 3, white sweetly scented, 8—9, fl
Comptonia peregrina, 2, foliage and bark pleasantly fragrant
Corylopsis glabrescens, 5, bright yellow flowers, 3-4

— spicata 6, as above
Cotinus coggygria, 5, crushed twigs smell of carrot
Crataegus, all, white, pink, red, very fragrant, May, fr
Cytisus praecox, 5, bright yellow, very fragrant, May, fl
Daphne spp., red-pink to white, strong, fl
Davidia involucrata, 6, leaves fragrant, fl
— — vilmoriana, 5, as above, fl
Deutzia gracilis, 4, flowers somewhat fragrant, May
Eleagnus spp. flowers very fragrant
Epigea repens, 2, light pink, very fragrant, April, #
*Eriobotrya japonica,*7, fragrant flowers, #
Eucalyptus spp., foliage and bark very fragrant
Euonymus sanguineus, 5, flowers greenish, fragrant, May
Fothergilla major, 5, white fully fragrant, May, fl
Franklinia alatamaha, 5, white, slightly fragrant, 9—10, fl
Fraxinus ornus, 5, white, slightly fragrant, May
Gaultheria procumbens, 3, white, 7—8, flowers, foliage and fruit aromatic, #
Hamamelis spp. yellow, slight fragrance, fl
Hypericum calycinum, 6, # foliage fragrant, fl
Jasminum officinale, 7, white, very fragrant, 6—8, fl
*— stephanense,*7, pink, more scented, 7—8, fl
Juglans nigra, 4, crushed foliage pungent, fr
— regia, 5, as above, fr
Juniperus spp. crushed foliage and fruit aromatic, #
Kalmia latifolia, 4, white-pink flowers slightly fragrant, #
Laburnum alpinum, 4, flowers yellow, slightly fragrant
Laurus nobilis, 6, # aromatic leaves used as seasoning
Lavendula angustifolia, 6, # blue flowers, whole plant fragrant, 7—8
— officinalis, 5, small lavender, fragrant plant, June, fl
Lindera benzoin, 4, foliage spicy scented
Lonicera caprifolium, zone 4, yellow with pink, strong, 6—7, fl fr
— fragrantissima, 5, cream flowers, strong fragrance, 2—3
— japonica, 4, # white flowers, sweet smelling, June
— purpusii, 4, cream, strong fragrance, 1—3
— standishii, 4, blooms white-yellow, strong scent, 1—3
— tibetica, 4, lilac flowers, 5—6
Magnolia kobus, 4, white, fragrant, 4—5, fl
— liliflora 'Nigra', 6, purple, good fragrance, 4—5, fl
— obovata, 5, pink-white, pleasant, May, fl
— sieboldii, 6, white,good fragrance, 6—7, fl
— soulangiana (and var.), 5, white with pink, good, 4—5, fl
— stellata, 5, white, slight fragrance, 3—4, fl
— tripetala, 5, large white, unpleasant scent, 5—6, fl
— virginiana, 5, # small but very fragrant, May, fl
Mahonia aquifolium, 5, yellow, fragrant 4—5 # fl fr
— bealii and japonica, 6, fragrant, 4—5 # fl fr
Malus spp. white, pink to purple, 4, 5—6, fl fr
Myrica gale, 2, crushed foliage pleasantly scented
— pensylvanica, 2, as above, (bayberry), fr
Melia azedarach, 7, lilac clusters, 4—5, fl fr
Osmanthus spp. flowers with good fragrance, #
Oxydendrum arboreum, 5, small white, slight fragrance, fl

Fragrant Plants

Paeonia suffruticosa, 5, white to red, some strong, May, fl
Paulownia tomentosa, 5, violet, fragrant, May, fl
Perovskia atriplicifolia, 4, flowers blue, foliage gray, aromatic, 8—9
Phellodendron, all, foliage aromatic, fr
Philadelphus, most very fragrant, fl
Pittosporum tobira, 8, cream-white, scented, May, fl
Populus balsamifera, 5, spring foliage has balsam scent
— *koreana*, 4, as above, very early leafing
— *trichocarpa*, 4, as above
Ptelea trifoliata, 4, flowers and foliage aromatic, fr
Prunus mume, 6, pink, red, white,very fragrant, 4—5, fl
— *padus*, white, strong fragrance, fl fr
— *serrulata* 'Amanogawa', 5, bright pink, slight scent, May, fl
— — 'Jonioi', white, slight almond scent, May, fl
— — 'Shirotae', white, fragrant, 4-5,fl
— *yedoensis*, 5, white with pink, fragrant, April, fl
Pterostyrax hispida, 5, white, fragrant, June, fl fr
Pyrus spp. flowers fragrant
Raphiolepis umbellata, zone 7, white, fragrant, May, fl
Rhododendron, many with fragrant flowers and foliage
— *calendulaceum*, 5, scarlet-orange, slight scent, 5-6, fl
— *fortunei*, 6, pink-white, strong and pleasant, # May, fl
— *luteum*, 6, (=Azalea pontica), yellow, good fragrance, May, fl
— *occidentale*, 6, pink-white, good, 5—6, fl
— *schlippenbachii*, 4, bright pink, good, 4—5, fl
— *viscosum*, 3, pink-white, good, 6—7, fl
— very manysmall leaved types with aromatic foliage
Rhus aromatica (=*R. canadensis*), 3, crushed foliage strong
Ribes americanum, 4, yellowish, flower and foliage aromatic, 4—5, fr
— *odoratum*, 4, reddish-yellow, very fragrant, May, fl
Robinia psuedoacacia, 3, white, fragrant, 5—6, fl
Rosa, see list p. 60
— *rubiginosa*, 5, foliage has strong apple scent, fl fr
Rosmarinus officinalis, 6, foliage very aromatic, #
Rubus odoratus, 3, pink-red, fragrant, 6—9, fl
Ruta graveolens, 4, dull yellow flower, foliage scented, 6—7
Sambucus, canadensis, 3, cream-white, soft fragrance, August, fl fr
— *nigra*, 5, white, foliage scented, June, fl fr
Santolina chamaecyparissus, 7, foliage very aromatic
*Sarcococca ruscifolia,*7, flowers white, fragrant, #
Sassafras albidum, 4, crushed foliage, roots, very aromatic
Skimmia japonica, 7, white, good fragrance, 4—5 # fr
Sophora japonica, 4, cream-white, slight fragrance, August, fl
Sorbus spp. white flowers slightly fragrant, fr
Spartium junceum, zone 7, bright yellow, good fragrance, fl
Styrax japonica, 5, white, slight scent, June, fl
Symplocos paniculata, 5, white, fragrant, 5—6, fl
Syringa, most species and varieties, see list p. 69, fl
— *vulgaris*, 3, lilac, very fragrant, May, fl
— *meyeri*, 5, light lilac, very fragrant, May, fl
Teucrium chamaedrys, 5, foliage fragrant, fl
Tilia europaea, 3, flowers small yellowish, very fragrant, 6—7

— *cordata*, 3, yellow, strong scented, June
— *tomentosa*, 4, yellow, very good scent, July
Vibrnum x burkwoodii, 5, white-pink, very good fragrance, May fl
— *carlcephalum*, 5, as above, fl
— *carlesii*, 4, as above, fl
— *farreri* (=fragrans) 5, flowers small pink-white, 1—3
— *bodnantense*, 6, as above, flowers much bigger, 1—3
Ulex europaeus, 6, yellow, fragrant, 5—6, fl
Umbellularia californica, 7, foliage aromatic when crushed, # fl
Vitex agnus castus,7, violet, flowers and foliage scented, 6—9
Vitis riparia (=odoratissima), 2, flowers green, very fragrant, June, fr
Wisteria floribunda, 4, lilac flowers, fragrant, 5—6
— *sinensis*, 5, lilac to violet, fragrant, 5—6, fl
Xanthoxylum, all, foliage aromatic when crushed, fr

5. Foliage Effects

a. Early Leafing Out

January, early February
   Lonicera purpusii, zone 4

Late February
   Alnus japonica, 4 of
   Corylus avellana and 'Aurea', 3 of

Early March
   Acer rubrum, 3
   Sorbaria arborea, 5
   Osmaronia cerasiformis, 7, light green new foliage

Late March
   Betula platyphylla (=mandschurica), 5, two to three weeks earlier
      than other Birches of
   Exochorda, all, bright green fl
   Larix gmelinii **var.** *japonica* (=L. kurilensis)|2
   Lonicera heckrottii, 4 fl
   Physocarpus opulifolius, 2, light green of
   — — 'Luteus', bright yellow of
   Prunus padus **var.** *commutata*, 3
   Ribes alpinum, 2
   Salix alba 'Tristis', 2 of
   Sambucus racemosa, 4 fr
   Sorbaria aitchisonii, 6 fl
   — *sorbifolia*, 2 fl
   Sorbus commixta, 5 of fr
   Spirea chamaedryfolia, 3 fl

Early Leafing

Early April
Acer velutinum, 5 of
Caragana arborescens, 2, yellowish green, of
Cercidiphyllum japonicum, 4 of
Cotoneaster multiflorus, 5 fl fr
Crataegus dahurica, 3 fr
Deutzia gracilis, 4, bright green, fl
Euonymus sachalinensis, 6 fr
Kerria japonica and 'Plenaflora', 4 fl
Larix decidua, 2
— *kaempferi* (=leptolepsis), 7
Paeonia suffruticosa, 5, red, fl
Potentilla fruticosa, 2, bright green, fl
Prinsepia sinensis, 4, bright green, fl
Populus koreana, 4 of
— *simonii*, 2 of
Prunus yedoensis, 5 fl
Rhododendron racemosum, 5, # fl
Sambucus nigra, 5 of fl fr
Spirea arguta, 4 fl
— *prunifolia*, 4 fl
— *thunbergii*, 4 fl
Syringa oblata, 3 fl
Viburnum lantana, 3 fl fr of
— *prunifolium*, 3 fl of

Late April
Azaleas
Cytisus kewensis, zone 6 fl
Betula, many types, of
Cytisus praecox, 5 fl
Malus baccata, 2 fl fr
— *floribunda*, 4 fl fr
— *halliana*, 5 fl fr
— *sargentii*, 5 fl fr
— *zumi*, 5 fl fr
Philadelphus coronarius, 4 fl
Prunus cerasifera (and var.), 3 fl fr of
— *serrulata* (and var.), 5 fl

(late April—early May most other plants leaf out, in middle to late May follow the Leguminosa and the rest)

b. The Major Broadleaf Evergreens
(Those species which hold their leaves through the winter but
drop them the following spring are noted with *)

Abelia grandiflora	zone 5		of fl ss
* *Akebia quinata*	4		of fl fr cl
Andromeda polifolia	2		fl of
Arctostaphylos uva-ursi	2		fr cr
Arundinaria simonii (Bamboo)	7		of su-ss
— *japonica*	6		of su-ss
— *murielae*	6		of su-ss
— *nitida*	6		of su-ss
Aucuba japonica	7		of fr ss
Berberis buxifolia	5		fl fr
—— 'Nana'			of fl
— *candidula*	5		of fl
— *darwinii*	7		of fl
— *gagnepainii var. lancifolia*	5		of fl su-sh
— *hybrido-gagnepainii* (and var.)	5		of fl su-sh
— *julianae*	5		of fl fr su-sh
* — *mentorensis*	5		fl fr su-sh
— *stenophylla*	5		fl fr su-sh
— *verruculosa*	5		fl of
Bruckenthalia spiculifolia	5		fl
Buxus sempervirens (and var.)	5		of su-sh
Buxus microphylla (and var.)	5		of su-sh
Calluna vulgaris, see list p. 50	4		
Camellia types			of fl
Cassiope tetragona	7		of fl
Choisya ternata	7		fl of
Cistus laurifolius	7		fl su
Cotoneaster congestus	6		of
— *conspicuus* and 'Decorus'	6		of
— *dammeri* with var. *radicans*	5		of cr
—— 'Skogholm'			
— *microphyllus*	5		of
—— *cochleatus* (=*melanotrichus*)			of cr
—— 'Ruby' (=*rubens*)			of
— *salicifolius*	6		of fl fr
—— *floccosus*			of cr
—— 'Gnom'			of cr
—— 'Parkteppich'			of cr
* — *watereri*	6		of fr
* —— 'Aldenhamensis'			of fl fr
* —— 'Cornubia'			of fl fr
* —— 'Pendulus'			of fl fr
Daboecia cantabrica	5		fl
Daphne cneorum	4		of fl cr
Dryas octopetala	4		of fl cr
Eleagnus ebbingei	6		of
— *pungens*	7		of

61

Broadleaf Evergreens

— — 'Simonii'		of
Empetrum nigrum	zone 2	cr
Erica, all, see list p. 40		
* *Escallonia* 'Donard Seedling'	7	fl
* *— virgata*	7	fl
Euonymus fortunei	5	of su-sh cr
— — 'Carrierei'		of fr su-sh
— — 'Coloratus'		of su-sh cr
— — 'Gracilis'		of su-sh cr
— — 'Minima'		su-sh cr
— — var. *radicans*		of su-sh cr
— — 'Reticulata'		of su-sh cr
— — 'Silver Gem'		of su-sh cl
— — 'Vegeta'		of fr su-sh
— japonicus (and var.)	8	of su-sh
Gaultheria miqueliana	5	of fr ss cr
— procumbens	3	of fr ss cr
— shallon	5	of fl fr ss
Hebe armstrongii	7	of
— buxifolia	7	of
— cupressoides	7	of
— glaucocoerulea	7	of
— hectori	7	of
Hedera colchica	5	of
— — *dentata* (=*amurense*)	5	of ss-sh cr
— helix	5	of ss-sh cr
Hedera helix 'Arborescens'	5	of ss-sh cr
— — 'Baltica'		of ss-sh cr
— — 'Conglomerata'		of ss-sh
— — 'Erecta' (= 'Minima')		of ss-sh
— — *hibernica*	5	of ss-sh cr
Hypericum calycinum	6	of fl su-sh
Iberis sempervirens (and var.)	5	fl
Ilex aquifolium	5	of fr su-sh
— — 'Camelliaefolia'		of su-sh
— — 'J.C. van Tol'		of fr su-sh
— — 'Heterophylla'		of su-sh
— — 'Pyramidalis'		of fr su-sh
— crenata	6	of su-sh
— — 'Convexa'		of su-sh
— glabra	3	of su-sh
— pedunculosa continentalis	5	of su-sh
— pernyi	6	of su-sh
yunnanensis	6	of su-sh
Kalmia angustifolia and 'Rubra'	2	fl ss
— latifolia	4	of fl ss
— polifolia	4	fl ss
Ledum groenlandicum	2	fl su
— palustre	2	fl su
Leiophyllum buxifolium	5	fl su
Leucothoe fontanesiana (=*catesbaei*)	4	of fl su-sh
Ligustrum ovalifolium	5	of

*	*Lonicera fragrantissima*	zone 5	fl
*	— *henryi*	4	of ss-sh cl
*	— *japonica*	4	of ss-sh cl
*	— — 'Aureo-reticulata'		of ss-sh cl
*	— — var. *halliana*		of ss-sh cl
	— *nitida*	7	of ss-sh
	— — 'Graziosa'		of ss-sh
	— — 'Elegant' (=*pileata yunnanensis*)		of ss-sh
*	— *purpusii*	4	fl
*¦	— *standishii*	4	fl
	Magnolia grandiflora	7	of fl
	— *virginiana*	5	of fl
	Mahoberberis neubertii	5	of
	Mahonia aquifolium	5	of fl fr su-sh
	— *bealii*	6	of fl fr su-sh
	— *japonica*	6	of fl fr su-sh
	— *repens*	5	of fl fr su-sh
*	*Myrica pensylvanica*	2	of fr
	Nandina domestica	7	of fl fr
	Osmanthus heterophyllus	6	of su
	Osmarea burkwoodii	6	of su
	Pachysandra terminalis and 'Variegata'	5	of su-sh cr
	Pernettya mucronata (and var.)	7	of fr
	Phillyrea vilmoriniana	6	of ss
	Phyllodoce coerulea	2	of fl
	Pieris forrestii	5	of fl ss
	— — 'Forest Flames', new foliage carmine	4	of fl ss
	— *floribunda*		of fl ss
	— *japonica*	5	of fl ss
	— — 'Red Mill', new foliage red		of fl ss
	— *taiwanensis*	7	of fl ss
	Prunus laurocerasus	6	of ss
	— — 'Mischeana'		of ss fl
	— — 'Schipkaensis'		of ss
	— — 'Schipkaensis Macrophylla'		of fl fr ss-sh
	— — 'Zabeliana'		of ss-sh
	— *lusitanica*	7	of fl fr
	Pyracantha coccinea	6	fl fr
	— — 'Kasan'		fl fr
	— — 'Lalandi'		fl fr
	— *crenulata* 'Rogersiana'	7	of fl fr
*	— *Quercus cerris* 'Ambrozyana'	6	of
*	— *hispanica*	6	of
	— *ilex*	7	of
	— *virginiana*	7	of
*	— *kewensis*	7	of
	Rhododendron see list p. 46		
*	*Rosa wichuriana*	5	fl cr
	Rubus henryi	6	of ss-sh cr
	Ruscus aculeatus	7	of fr ss
	Santolina chamaecyparissus	7	of
	Sarcococca ruscifolia	7	of ss-sh

Red Foliage

Skimmia japonica	zone 7	of fr ss
— *reveesiana* 'Rubella'	7	of fr ss
Stranvaesia davidiana	6	of fl ss
Teucrium 'chamaedrys'	5	of fr su-ss
Trochodendron aralioides	6	of
* *Ulmus parvifolia*	5	of su-ss
Vaccinium vitis-idaea	2	of
* *Viburnum burkwoodii*	5	fl ss
— *davidii*	7	fl ss fr of
* — *henryi*	7	of fl ss
* — *juddii*	5	of fl
— *rhytidophyllum*	5	of fl fr su-ss
— *tinus*	7	of fl fr su-ss
Vinca major	7	of fl su-ss
— *minor* (and var.)	4	fl su-sh cr
Yucca filamentosa	4	of fl su
* *Zenobia pulverulenta*	5	fl ss-sh

c. Colorful Foliage

Red Foliage

DECIDUOUS

Acer campestre 'Schwerinii'	zone 5	of su
— *cappadocicum* 'Rubrum'	5	of su
— *palmatum* 'Atropurpureum'	5	of su-ss
— — 'Ornatum' (— 'Dissectum Purpureum')		of su-ss
— *platanoides* 'Crimson King'	3	of fl su
— — 'Schwedleri'		of fl su
— *pseudoplatanus* 'Purpurascens'	5	of su
Actinidia kolomikta, leaves pink-white	4	of su-ss cl
Berberis ottawensis 'Superba'	4	of fl su
— *thunbergii* 'Atropurpurea'	4	of fl fr su
— — 'Atropurpurea Nana'		of su
— — 'Rosy Glow'		of su
Betula pendula 'Purpurea'	2	of su
Corylus avellana 'Fusco-rubra'	3	of e su-ss
— *maxima* 'Atropurpurea'	4	of e su-ss
Fagus silvatica 'Riversii'	4	of su
— — 'Pendula Purpurea'		of su
Cotinus coggygria 'Royal Purple'	5	of fl su
Clematis montana 'Rubens'	5	of fl su-ss cl
Malus x 'Profusion'	4	of fl fr su
— *x* 'Royalty'	4	of fl fr su
— (*purpurea*) 'Lemoinei'	4	of fl fr su

Prunus blireana	zone 5	of fl su
— *cerasifera* 'Nigra'	3	of fl su
— — 'Atropurpurea'		of fl su
— — 'Woodi'		of fl su
— *cistena*	2	of fl su
— *padus* 'Colorata'	3	of fl su-ss
— *persica* 'Rubrifolia'	5	of fl fr su
Rosa rubrifolia	2	of su
Quercus robur 'Purpurea'	5	of su
Ulmus glabra 'Atropurpurea'	4	of su
— *procera* 'Purpurea'	5	of su
Weigela florida 'Purpurea'	5	of su

EVERGREENS

The red color in evergreens is often a red-brown and usually only found in the new spring growth or the winter coloration.

Thuja occidentalis, winter color red-brown,	zone 2	su
— — 'Beteramsii, in summer brown-green		su
Cryptomeria japonica, in winter somewhat brown	5	su-ss
— — 'Elegans', in winter good red-brown		su-ss
Juniperus horizontalis, winter purple-violet	3	of su cr
— — 'Plumosa', as above		of su cr
— *virginiana* 'Reptans', as above although not as intensive	2	of su cr

Yellow Foliage

BROADLEAVES

Acer campestre 'Postelense'	zone 5	of su
— *japonicum* 'Aureum'	5	of su
— *negundo* 'Odessanum'	2	of su
— *palmatum dissectum* 'Flavescens'	5	of su
— *pseudoplatanus* 'Leopoldii'	5	of su
— — 'Worleei'		of su
— *saccharinum* 'Lutescens'	3	of su
Alnus incana 'Aurea'	2	of fl fr su
Berberis thunbergii 'Aurea'	4	of su
Buxus sempervirens 'Aurea'	5	su-sh #
Calluna vulgaris 'Aurea' and 'Caprea'	4	of su #
Catalpa bignonioides 'Aurea'	4	of su
Cornus alba 'Spaethii'	2	of su-ss
Corylus avellana 'Aurea'	3	of su-ss
Euonymus fortunei Aureo Marginata'	5	of su-ss #
— — 'Aureo Variegata'		of su-ss #
Fagus silvatica 'Zlatia' (young foliage)	4	of su
— — 'Aureo-pendula'		of su
Fraxinus excelsior 'Aurea' (weak grower)	3	of su
— — 'Jaspidea' (strong growing)		of su
Gleditsia triacanthos inermis 'Sunburst'	4	of su
Hebe armstrongii	6	of su-ss

Yellow Foliage

Hedera helix 'Aureo-variegata'	zone 5	of su-sh
Ilex aquifolium 'Golden King'	5	# of fr ss
— — 'Golden Queen' (fruitless)		of ss
Laburnum anagyroides 'Aureum'	5	of fl
Ligustrum ovalifolium 'Aureum'	5	of
— x *vicaryi*	4	of
Lonicera japonica 'Aureo-reticulata'	4	of ss cr
Philadelphus coronarius 'Aureus'	4	of
Physocarpus opulifolius 'Luteus'	2	of
Populus alba 'Richardii'	3	of
— *canadensis* 'Aurea'	4	of
Ptelea trifoliata 'Aurea'	4	of
Quercus robur 'Concordia'	5	of
Robinia pseudoacacia 'Frisia'	3	of
Sambucus nigra 'Lutea'	5	of
— *canadensis* 'Aurea'	3	of
— *racemosa* 'Ornata'	4	of
Sorbus aria 'Lutescens'	5	of fr
— *aucuparia* 'Dirkenii'	2	of fr
Ulmus carpinifolia 'Wredii'	4	of
— *procera* 'Vanhouttei'	5	of
Viburnum opulus 'Aureum'	3	of fl fr

EVERGREENS

Abies procera 'Aurea'	zone 5	of
Cedrus atlantica 'Aurea'	6	of
— — 'Pendula Aurea'		of
— *deodar* 'Aurea'	6	of
Chamaecyparis lawsoniana 'Lane' (='Lanei Aurea')	5	of
— — 'Stewartii'		of
— *nootkatensis* 'Lutea'	4	of
— *obtusa* 'Aurea'	3	of
— — 'Nana Aurea'		of
— — 'Tetragona Aurea'		of
— — 'Crippsii'		of
— *pisifera* 'Aurea'	3	of
— — 'Filifera Aurea'		of
— — 'Mops'		of
— — 'Nana Lutea'		of
— — 'Plumosa Aurea'		of
Juniperus chinensis 'Pfitzeriana Aurea'	4	of
— — 'Gold Coast'		of
— — 'Plumosa Aurea'		of
— *communis* 'Depressa Aurea'	2	of
Picea abies 'Aurea'	5	of
— *orientalis* 'Aureospica'	4	of
Taxus baccata 'Adpressa Aurea'	6	of su-ss
— — 'Dovastoniana Aurea'		of su-ss
— — 'Fastigiata Aurea'		of su-ss
— — 'Repandens Aurea'		of su-ss

— — 'Semperaurea'			of su-ss
— — 'Washingtonii'			of su-ss
— *cuspidata* 'Aurescens'		4	of
Thuja occidentalis 'Aurea'		2	of
— — 'Rheingold'			of
— *orientalis* Aurea Nana'		6	of
— *plicata* 'Variegata'			of

Gray to Silver-gray or Blue-gray Foliage

BROADLEAVES

Acer saccharinum	zone 3	of	underside of leaf whitish
Andromeda polifolia	2	of #	bluish upper, white lower leaf surface
Artemesia abrotanum	5	of su	gray-green
Caryopteris x clandonensis	5	of fl	gray-green
Colutea orientalis	6	of fl	gray to blue-green
Elaeagnus angustifolia	2	of su fr	silver-gray foliage
— *umbellatus*	3	of su fr	silvery cast
Eucalyptus globulus	9	of su	white young leaves
— *leucoxylon*	9	of su	gray-green foliage
Fagus engleriana	5	of	blue-green
Hippophae rhamnoides	3	of fr	silvery cast
Lavandula, all		of fl	silver-gray to gray-green
Lonicera korolkowii (and var.)	5	of su fl	striking blue-green
Olea europaea	9	# su	gray-green, silvery beneath
Perovskia atriplicifolia	4	of su fl	silver-gray leaves
Pyrus salicifolia	4	of su	silver-gray, pendulous
Populus alba	3	of su	underside of leaf snow white
Santolina chamaecyparissus	7	of su	whitish gray, tomentose
Salix alba 'Argentea'	2	of su	foliage silver-gray
— *repens* 'Argentea'	4	of su	as above
Salvia officinalis	4	of su	gray-green
Shepherdia argentea	2	of e	silvery foliage
Sorbus aria (and var.)	5	of fr	undersides whitish
Tamarix pentandra	2	of su fl	blue-green foliage
Tilia petiolaris	5	of	undersides white tomentose
— *tomentosa*	4	of	as above
Zenobia pulverulenta	5	of fl	whitish glaucous leaves

EVERGREEN

Abies concolor (and var.)	zone 4	of	blue-gray to whitish
— *lasiocarpa arizonica*	2	of	
— *pinsapo* 'Glauca'	6	of	
— *procera* 'Glauca'	5	of	
Cedrus atlantica 'Glauca'	6	of	
— *deodara*	7	of	most blue-green
Chamaecyparis lawsoniana 'Alumni'	5	of	
— — 'Columnaris'		of	

White Foliage

— — 'Glauca Argentea'		of	
— — 'Ellwoodii'		of	
— — 'Fletcheri'		of	
— · — 'Oregon Blue'		of	
— — 'Robusta Glauca'		of	
— — 'Silver Queen'		of	
— — 'Minima Glauca'		of	low, wide
— — 'Triumph van Boskoop'		of	
— *pisifera* 'Boulevard'			
(= 'Cyanoviridis')	3	of	steel blue, soft
— — 'Squarrosa'		of	blue-green, larger
Cunninghamia lanceolata 'Glauca'	5	of	glaucous foliage
Juniperus chinensis 'Blaauwi'	4	of	blue-green
— — 'Hetzii'		of	upright
— — 'Gray Owl'		of	broad
— *communis* 'Compressa'	2	of	dwarf
— — var. *montana*		of	wide, flat
— *horizontalis* (and var.)	3	of cr	prostrate
— *scopulorum* (and var.)	5	of	
— *squamata* 'Meyeri'	4	of	very blue, upright
— *virginiana* 'Burkii'	2	of	blue-gray, columnar
— — 'Glauca'		of	wide habit
— — 'Pyramidalis Glauca'		of	blue, columnar
— — 'Skyrocket'		of	very blue, 5m high 30 cm diameter
Picea asperata 'Glauca'	5	of	nice blue
— *englemannii* 'Argentea'	2	of	silver-gray
— — 'Glauca'		of	steel blue
— *glauca*	2	of	blue-green
— — 'Echiniformis'		of	half round, blue-gray
— *mariana* 'Nana'	2	of	broadly conical, bluish
— *pungens* 'Glauca' types			
('Hoopsi', 'Moerheim', 'Koster', 'Globosa, etc.)			
Pinus pumila	4	of	
— *parviflora* 'Glauca'	5	of	
— *silvestris* 'Watereri'	2	of	
Pseudotsuga menziesii 'Glauca'	5	of	
Tsuga mertensiana 'Glauca'	5	of	

White Foliage

BROADLEAVES

Acer negundo 'Variegatum	zone 2	of su-ss
— *platanoides* 'Drummondii'	3	of su-ss
Actinidia kolomikta	4	of cl
Aralia elata 'Argenteo-variegata'	3	of fl su
Cornus mas 'Variegata'	4	of su-ss
Crataegus oxycantha 'Gireoudii'	4	of su
Euonymus fortunei 'Silver Queen'	5	of su-ss cl #
— *japonicus* 'Albo-marginatus'	8	of su-ss #

Hedera canariensis		
'Gloire de Marengo'	zone 7	of ss cr #
Hibiscus syriacus 'Variegatus'	5	of fr ss #
Ilex aquifolium 'Albomarginata'	5	of fr ss #
— — 'Silver Queen'		of ss fruitless #
Kerria japonica 'Picta'	4	of fl
Ligustrum ovalifolium		
'Aurgenteo-variegatum'	5	of
Pieris japonica 'Variegata'	5	of ss #
Pachysandra terminalis		
'Variegata'	5	of ss #
Pittosporum tobira 'Variegata'	8	of su fl #
Quercus petraea		
'Argenteo-variegata'	4	of
Sambucus nigra		
'Argenteo-marginata'	5	of
Sasa veitchii	6	of ss (bamboo)
Vinca minor 'Variegata'	4	of fl #
Weigela florida 'Nana Variegata'	5	of fl su

EVERGREEN

Chamaecyparis lawsoniana		
'Albo-spica'	5	of
— *obtusa* 'Maresii'	3	of
— *pisifera* 'Plumosa Argentea'	3	of
Juniperus chinensis 'Variegata'	4	of
Tsuga canadensis 'Albo-spica'	4	of
Thujopsis dolabrata 'Variegata'	6	of

d. Effective Autumn Foliage

(of = most outstanding types)
Fall colors will vary somewhat from year to year depending upon the weather. The best color is brought about by consecutive cold nights and sunny days. Those varieties selected for attractive fall foliage can be just as effective as flower or fruit color. (The symbol **fr** followed by a color indicates the color of the ripened fruit.)

Acer campestre, zone 5	tree, large shrub	yellow
— *capillipes,* 6	tree	red
— *cappadocicum,* 5	tree	yellow
— *circinatum,* 5	tree, shrub	red of
— *cissifolium,* 6	tree	pink-red of
— *davidii,* 6	shrub	yellow-red
— *ginnala,* 2	large shrub	fire red of
— *grosseri hersii,* 6	large shrub	red

Autumn Color

— *japonicum*		
'Aconitifolium' zone 5	shrub	bright orange of
— — 'Aureum'	shrub	gold-yellow
— *macrophyllum*, 6	tree	yellow-orange
— *mono*, 5	tree	gold-yellow
— *negundo*, 2	tree	yellow
— *nikoense*, 5	tree	carmine of
— *opalus obtusatum*, 5	tree	bright yellow
— *palmatum*, 5	small tree	carmine
— — 'Dissectum'	shrub	orange
— — 'Ornatum'	shrub	red
— *pensylvanicum*, 3	tree	yellow
— *platanoides*, 3	tree	yellow-orange
— — 'Crimson King'	tree	copper red
— — 'Faassen's Black'	tree	black-red
— — 'Schwedleri'	tree	copper red
— *psuedoplatanus*, 5	tree	gold-yellow of
— *rubrum* (and var.), 3	tree	bright red of
— *rufinerve*, 5	tree	dark yellow
— *saccharinum*, 3	tree	yellow
— — 'Wieri'	tree	yellow
— *saccharum*, 3	tree	bright salmon yellow
— *spicatum*, 2	large shrub	red to yellow
— *tataricum*, 4	large shrub	red and yellow of
— *triflorum*, 5	small tree	orange-red
Aesculus, most	tree	yellow-brown
— *parviflora*, 4	shrub	lemon yellow
Actinidia arguta, 4	vine	bright yellow
Akebia quinata, 4	vine	purple-brown
Amelanchier, all	small trees	orange to red of
Aronia, all	shrubs	scarlet red
Azalea, all	shrubs	yellow to red
Berberis koreana, 5	small shrub	orange red of, fr red
— *mentorensis*, 5	small shrub	scarlet and green
— *thunbergii*, 4	small shrub	orange-red, fr red
— — 'Atropurpurea'	small shrub	carmine red, fr red
— *wilsoniae*, 5	small shrub	red, fr red
Betula, most	trees	yellow
— *maximowicziana*, 5	tree	gold-yellow of
— *medwediewii*, 4	shrub	brown-yellow
Callicarpa, all	shrubs	yellow and lilac, fr lilac
Calluna vulgaris 'Aurea', 4	small shrub	bronze-yellow
— — 'Cuprea'	small shrub	coppery
Carpinus betulus, 4	tree	yellow
— *caroliniana*, 2	tree	red and orange of
Carya, all	trees	yellow of
Castanea sativa, 5	tree	bright yellow of
Catalpa bignonioides, 4	tree	yellow
Cercidiphyllum japonicum, 4	tree	salmon pink
Cercis canadensis, 4	tree	yellow
Chionanthus spp.	shrub	good yellow
Cladrastis lutea, 3	tree	gold yellow of

Clethra barbinervis, zone 5	shrub	red and yellow
— *alnifolia*, 3	shrub	bright yellow
Cornus alba, 2	shrub	pink, on red bark
— — 'Sibirica'	shrub	as above, better bark
— *amomum*, 5	shrub	red
— *florida*, 4	small tree	violet red
— *kousa* and var. *chinensis*	small tree	scarlet red
— *mas*, 4	shrub	yellow-orange
— *nuttallii*, 7	tree	yellow to red
— *racemosa*, 4	shrub	purple
— *sanguinea*, 4	shrub	red
Corylopsis, all	shrub	mostly yellow
Corylus americana, 4	shrub	red-brown
— all others	shrub	yellow
Cotinus coggygria, 5	shrub	yellow to scarlet
Cotoneaster acutifolius, 4	shrub	red, fr red
— *adpressus*, 4	shrub	dull red, fr red
— *bullatus*, 5	shrub	red, fr red
— *dielsianus*, 5	shrub	red, fr red
— *divaricatus*, 5	shrub	orange, fr red
— *horizontalis*, 4	shrub	scarlet of, fr orange-red
— *praecox*, 4	shrub	bright red, fr red
— *multiflorus*, 5	shrub	brown, fr dark red
Crataegus coccinea, 5	shrub	yellow to orange of
— *crus-galli*, 4	shrub	yellow with pink of
— *lavallei*, 4	small tree	brown red-orange of
— *nitida*, 4	small tree	orange and red
— *phaenopyrum*, 4	small tree	orange-red of
Decaisnea fargesii, 6	shrub	yellow
Deutzia scabra, 5	shrub	yellow
Dirca palustris, 4	shrub	yellow-green
Disanthus cercidifolius, 6	shrub	wine red of
Enkianthus campanulatus, 4	shrub	scarlet and yellow of
Euonymus alatus, 3	shrub	carmine of
— *bungeanus*, 4	shrub	pale yellow to pink
— *europaeus*, 3	shrub	yellow and red
— *latifolius*, 5	shrub	carmine of
— *sanguineus*, 5	shrub	brown-red
— *sachalinensis*, 5	shrub	yellow of
Fagus grandifolia, 3	tree	red-brown
— *silvatica*, 4	tree	brown to yellow-brown
Forsythia viridissima, 5	small shrub	yellow to purple
Fothergilla all	small shrub	most orange and red
Franklinia alatamaha, 5	shrub	crimson
Fraxinus americana, 3	tree	reddish
— — 'Acuminata'	tree	violet red and gray of
— — 'Autumn Purple'	tree	deep purple of
— *excelsior*, 3	tree	yellow
— — 'Aurea'	tree	gold yellow of
— *ornus*, 5	tree	yellow
— *pensylvanica*, 3	tree	gold yellow or green
Gingko biloba, 4	tree	clear yellow of

Autumn Color

Gymnocladus dioecus, zone 4	tree	bright yellow
Hamamelis japonica, 4	shrub	yellow of
— *virginiana*, 4	shrub	bright yellow of
— *mollis*, 5	shrub	orange of
Halesia carolina, 4	small tree	yellow
Hydrangea quercifolia, 5	shrb	deep maroon red
— *macrophylla*, 5	shrub	red brown to red
Itea virginica, 5	shrub	red and orange
Juglans, all	trees	greenish-yellow
Kalopanax pictus, 4	tree	red
Kerria japonica, 5	shrub	yellow
Larix, most	trees	gold yellow of
Koelreuteria paniculata, 5	tree	orange-yellow
Leucothoe fontanesiana, 4	shrub	wine red all winter
Lindera, all	shrub	yellow
Ligustrum obtusum regelianum, 3	shrub	violet brown
Liquidambar styraciflua, 5	tree	red-orange-yellow of
Liriodendron tulipifera, 4	tree	yellow of
Maackia amurensis, 4	tree	yellow
Maclura pomifera, 4	tree	yellow
Magnolia, most	tree or shrub	yellow-brown
Mahonia aquifolium, 5	shrub	reddish
Malus coronaria, 4	small tree	dark red-orange of
— 'Cowichan'	large shrub	red to orange
— 'Red Tip'	large shrub	red to orange
— 'Wabiskaw'	large shrub	red to orange
Malus tschonoskii, 5	tree	carmine red of
Menispermum canadense, 4	vine	bright yellow
Mespilus germanica, 5	small tree	orange to gold brown
Metasequoia glyptostroboides, 5	tree	gold brown
Morus alba, 4	tree	yellow
Nandina domestica, 7	small shrub	wine red of
Nyssa, all	trees	scarlet to yellow of
Oxydendrum arboreum, 5	small tree	bright red of
Parrotia persica, 5	large shrub	scarlet with violet of
Parthenocissus	vines	red to carmine of
Phellodendron, all	trees	green-yellow
Physocarpus opulifolius, 2	shrub	gold-yellow
Photinia villosa, 4	shrub	bright red of
Platanus, all	trees	yellow-brown
Poncirus trifoliata, 6	shrub	yellow
Populus, all	trees	yellow to brown
Prunus avium, 3	tree	yellow to red of
— *maximowiczii*, 4	tree	scarlet
— *padus*, 3	tree	yellow to red
— *serotina*, 3	tree	yellow
— *sargentii*, 4	tree	yellow of
— *serrulata*, 5	trree	orange-yellow of
Pterocarya, all	trees	green-yellow to brown
Quercus alba, 4	tree	violet-red of

Quercus bicolor, zone 3	tree	bright yellow
— *coccinea*, 4	tree	orange to scarlet
— *imbricaria*, 5	tree	dark brown and red
— *palustris*, 4	tree	red or yellow of
— *petraea*, 4	tree	leather brown
— *robur*, 5	tree	yellow-brown
— *rubra*, 4	tree	scarlet red of
— *shumardii*, 5	tree	red-brown
— most others	tree	leather brown
Pyrus, most	trees	yellow-green or red
Rhamnus, all	large shrubs	yellow to brown
Rhododendron (Azaleas)	shrubs	
— yellow flowering types		most bright yellow of
— white flowering types		most bright yellow of
— pink and red types		orange to bright red of
Rhus aromatica, 3	shrub	red
— *glabra* (and var.), 2	large shrub	scarlet of
— *typhina* (and var.), 5	large shrub	scarlet-orange of
— *vernicifera*, 5	large shrub	yellow
Ribes floridum, 5	shrub	red and yellow
— *odoratum*, 4	shrub	scarlet
— *sanguineum*, 5	shrub	green-yellow
Rosa multiflora, 5	shrub	yellow
— *nitida*, 3	shrub	bronze brown of
— *rugosa*, 2	shrub	orange-red to yellow of
— *virginiana*, 3	shrub	red-brown to orange
Rubus, all	shrubs	most yellow
Sassafras albidum, 4	tree	yellow to orange
Sorbus, Aucuparia group (pinnate leaves)	most trees	red to carmine of
— *Aria* group (simple leaves)	trees	most leather brown
— *alnifolia*, 4	tree	red, consistent
— *sargentiana*, 6	small tree	orange with red of
Spirea albiflora, 4	small shrub	yellow
— *bumalda*	small shrub	red to brown of
— *prunifolia*, 4	shrub	brown to violet-brown
— *thunbergii*, 4	small shrub	red
— *vanhouttei*, 4	shrub	red to carmine of
— others	shrubs	most red or yellow-green
Stephanandra, all	shrubs	red-yellow of
Stewartia, all	small trees	bright red to orange
Stranvaesia davidiana, 7	shrub	some red, yellow or green
Symphoricarpos, all	shrubs	most yellow
Syringa oblata, 3	shrub	wine red, early of
— others	shrubs	most yellow to brown
Taxodium distichum, 4	tree	brown to red-brown of
Tilia, most	trees	yellow
— *tomentosa*, 4	tree	green
Ulmus, all	trees	yellow
Vaccinium corymbosum, 3	shrub	carmine of

Red Fruit

Viburnum carlesi, zone 4	shrub	wine red
— *dilatatum*, 5	shrub	russet red
— *lentago*, 2	shrub	purple-red of
— *molle*, 3	shrub	reddish
— *opulus*, 3	shrub	deep red of
— *plicatum*, 4	shrub	dark brown-red
— *prunifolium*, 3	shrub	purple-red of
— *rufidulum*, 5	shrub	red
— *setigerum*, 5	shrub	orange-yellow
— *sieboldii*, 4	shrub	red
— *trilobum*, 2	shrub	red
Vitis amurensis, 4	vine	purple
— *coignetiae*, 5	vine	scarlet of
— *vinifera*, 4	vine	orange to scarlet
Xanthoceras sorbifolium, 5	large shrub	greenish-yellow
Zelkova, most	trees	yellow-brown
Zenobia pulverulenta, 5	small shrub	yellow and red or brown

6. Fruit Character

(In order by color and months effective)

RED FRUIT

Daphne mezereum	6	.	.	.	.	.	.	.	.	fl zone 4	poisonous
Eleagnus multiflora	6	.	.	.	.	.	.	.	.	of 4	edible
Acer ginnala	.	7	8	9	.	.	.	.	.	of 2	
— *tataricum*	.	7	8	.	.	.	.	.	.	of 4	
Amelanchier *canadensis*	.	7	.	.	.	.	.	.	.	e 4	
Cornus mas	.	7	8	.	.	.	.	.	.	e 4	
Lonicera deflexicalyx	.	7	8	.	.	.	.	.	.	5	with large white calyx
— *tatarica* (and var.)	.	7	8	.	.	.	.	.	.	fl 3	
Rhus typhina	.	7	8	9	to March	.				fl of 5	sumac 'tea'
Rosa carolina	.	7	o	.	.	.	.	.	.	fl of 4	
— *pendulina* (= *alpina*)	.	7	8	.	.	.	.	.	.	fl 5	
— *rugosa*	.	7	8	.	.	.	.	.	.	fl e 2	(rose hips)
Sambucus racemosa	.	7	8	.	.	.	.	.	.	fl 4	
Shepherdia canadensis	.	7	.	.	.	.	.	.	.	e 2	
Acer macrophyllum	.	.	8	9	.	.	.	.	.	of 6	
— *pseudoplatanus* 'Erythrocarpum'	.	.	8	9	.	.	.	.	.	5	red wings
Berberis, most deciduous types	.	.	8	9	10	.	.	.	.	fl	

Plant	8	9	10	11	12	1	2	Notes	
— koreana	8	9	10	til spring				zone 5	
Cotoneaster dammeri	8	9	10	11	.	.		fl cr # 5	
— divaricatus	8	9	10	11	.	.	.	fl 5	
— franchetii	8	9	10	11	.	.	.	fl 6	
— microphyllus	8	9	10	11	12	1	2	# 5	
— multiflorus	8	9	.	.	.	.	.	fl 5	
— racemiflorus	8	9	.	.	.	.	.		
Crataegus coccinea	8	9	10	11	12	1	.	fl 5	
— monogyna	8	9	10	.	.	.	.	fl 4	
Euonymus europaeus	8	9	10	11	12	.	.	fl u 3	
Ilex pernyi	8	9	.	.	.	.	.	u #|6	
Lonicera korolkowii	8	.	.	.	.	.	.	fl 5	
— maackii	8	9	10	11	12	.	.	fl 2	
— xylosteum	8	9	.	.	.	.	.	fl u 4	
Lycium, all	8	9	.	.	.	.	.	fl cr cl	
Malus atrosanguinea	8	9	10	0	0	0	0	fl	
— baccata jackii	8	9	10	11	12	0	0	fl 4	brown-red
— purpura **'Aldenhamensis'**	8	9	10	.	.	.	.	fl 4	
— x 'Lemoinei'	8	9	10	.	.	.	.	fl 4	
Ribes alpinum	8	.	.	.	.	.	.	fl 2	
Rosa rubiginosa	8	9	10	11	.	.	.	fl 5	
— multiflora	8	9	10	11	12	1	2	fl 5	
— rubrifolia	8	9	.	.	.	.	.	fl 2	
— virginiana		9	10	11	12	1	2 |	cf fl 3	
Rubus odoratus	8	.	.	.	.	.	.	fl u 3	
— phoenicolasius	8	.	.	.	.	.	.	fl u 5	
Sambucus canadensis	8	9	.	.	.	.	.	fl 3	
Sorbus aucuparia	8	9	.	.	.	.	.	fl 2	
Viburnum opulus	8	9	10	11	12	1	.	fl 3	
— sargentii	8	9	10	11	12	1	.	fl 4	
Aronia arbutifolia		9	10	11	12	.	.	fl 4	
Berberis thunbergii		9	10	11	12—3			fl 4	
Cotoneaster apiculata		9	10	11	.	.	.	4	
— henryanus		9	.	.	.	.	.	fl 7	
— conspicuus		9	10	.	.	.	.	# 6	
— horizontalis		9	10	11	.	.	.	fl 4	
— salicifolius floccosus		9	10	11	.	.	.	fl # 6	
— watereri		9	10	11	12	.	.	7	
— — **'Cornubia'**		9	10	11	12	.	.		
— — **'Pendulus'**		9	10	11	12	.	.		
Crataegus crus-galli		9	10	11	12	1	2	fl 4	
— lavallei		9	10	11	12	.	.	fl 4	
Euonymus americanus		9	10	11	.	.	.	of 6	
— bungeanus sempersistens		9	10	11	12	.	.	of 4	
— fortunei **'Vegetus'**		9	10	11	12	.	.	# 5	
— latifolius		9	10	.	.	.	.	of 5	
— sanguineus		9	10	.	.	.	.	of 5	
— yedoensis		9	10	11	.	.	.	of 4	
Gaultheria procumbens		9	10	11	12—3			of fl # 3	

Yellow-Orange Fruit

	Months	Notes
Hippophae rhamnoides	9 10 11 12—3	of #|zone 5
—— 'J.C. van Tol'	9 10 11 12	#
—— 'Pyramidalis'	9 10 11 12	#
— *serrata*	9 10 11	u 5
— *verticillata*	9 10 11 12	uf 3
Leycesteria formosa	9 10	zone 7
Lonicera alpigena	9	fl 5
Magnolia lilliflora	9	fl u 5
Malus 'Redflesh'	9	fl
— *sargentii*	9 10 11	fl 5
Nandina domestica	9 10 11 12 1 2	of ss # 7
Pernettya mucronata	9 10 11 12 1 2	# 7
Photinia villosa	9 10	fl of 4
Pyracantha coccinea 'Kasan'	9 10 11 12	fl of # 5
—— 'Orange Glow'	9 10 11 12	fl of # 6
Rosa canina	9 10 11 12	fl 3
— *hugonis*	9	fl 5
— *moyesii*	9 10	fl 5
— *setigera*	9 10 11 12 1 2	fl 4
Skimmia japonica	9 10 11 12—4	of # 7
Sorbus americana	9 10	fl of 2
— *aria*	9 10	fl of 5
— *hybrida*	9 10	fl of 4
— *sargentiana*	9 10	fl of 6
— *vilmorinii*	9 10	of 5 — red fading to pink
Symphoricarpos chenaultii	9 10 11	of 4
Viburnum wrightii	9 10 11	of 5
Ailanthus altissima 'Erythrocarpum'	10	of 4
Cotoneaster simonsii	10	of 5
Euonymus alatus	10	of 3
Stranvaesia davidiana	10 11 12 1	of # 7
Symphoricarpos orbiculatus	10 11 12	2
—— 'Erect'	10 11 12	2
—— 'Magic Berry'	10 11 12	

YELLOW TO YELLOW-ORANGE FRUIT

	Months	Notes	
Daphne mezereum 'Album'	6	fl 4	poisonous!
Malus baccata	8 9 10 11	fl 2	also red
— *floribunda*	8 9 10	fl 4	also with red
— *sieboldii* 'Wintergold'	8 9 10 11 12	|fl 5	yellow
— *toringoides*	8 9 10 11 12	fl 5	yellow with red
— *zumi*	8 9 10 11	fl 5	brownish
—— *calocarpa*	8 9 10 11 12	fl 5	orange

	6	7	8	9	10	11	12	1	2	3		
Poncirus trifoliata			8	9	10	11	12				fl zone 6	lemon-yellow
Viburnum opulus												
'Xanthocarpum'			8	9	10	11	12	1	2	3	fl 3	orange
Asimina triloba				9	10						of e 5	green-yellow
Chaenomeles, types				9	10	11	12	1			fl F	gold-yellow
Cydonia oblonga				9	10						fl 4	quince
Eleagnus angustifolia				9							of 3	orange
Hippophae rhamnoides				9	10	11					e of 3	orange
Ilex aquifolium'												
'Bacciflava'				9	10	11	12	1	2	3	# 5	
Malus arnoldiana				9	10						fl 4	yellow and red
Sorbus aucuparia												
'Xanthocarpa'				9	10						of 2	
Celastrus, most					10	11					cl	red and yellow

BLUE FRUIT

	6	7	8	9	10	11	12		
Lonicera coerulea	6	7						of fl 6	
Juniperus virginiana									
'Canaertii'		7	8	9	10	11—3		#2	
Mahonia aquifolium		7						u # 5	
— bealei		7						u # 6	
Amelanchier lamarckii									
(=x grandiflora)	6	7						e fl 4	
— ovalis			8					e fl u 4	
— stolonifera	6	7						e fl u 4	
Berberis gagnepainii			8	9	10			# u 5	
— julianae			8	9	10			# u 5	
— verruculosa			8	9	10			# u 5	
Clerodendrum									
trichotomum			8	9				F 6	
Cornus amomum			8	9	10	11—3		5	
Prunus spinosa			8	9	10	11		e fl 4	
Sambucus coerulea			8					3 fl S H 5	
Vaccinium corymbosum			8					3	
Ampelopsis									
aconitifolia				9	10			cl 4	
— brevipedunculata				9	10			cl 4	
Chionanthus virginica				9				fl cf 4	
Decaisnea fargesii				9				of 6	
Juniperus communis				9	10—3			# 2	
Parthenocissus, all				9	10.			of cl	
Symplocos paniculata				9				fl 5	
Viburnum davidii				9	10			fl of # 7	
— dentatum				9	10			fl 2	
Vitis vinifera				9	10			e 4	
Lonicera pileata					10	11	12	cr # 5	
— nitida 'Elegant'					10	11	12	# 7	

White or Black Fruit

BLACK FRUIT

	4	5	6	7	8	9	10	11	12	1	2		
Hedera helix	4	5	6									u # zone 5	
Empetrum nigrum			6	7	8	9						cr # 2	
Lonicera involucrata			6	7	8							fl 6	
Ilex glabra				7	8	9	10—2					of # 3	
Lonicera ledebourii				7	8	9						of fl 4	
Prunus padus				7	8							fl 3	red at first
— *virginiana*				7	8							fl 2	red at first
Viburnum cassinoides				7	8	9						of 2	red and black
— *lantana*				7	8	9						of 3	red and black
— *rhytidophyllum*				7	8	9						of # 5	red and black
Cotoneaster melanocarpus					8							4	
Hypericum androsaemum					8	9	10	11				fl 4	
Ilex crenata					8	9	10	11	12			u # 6	
Ligustrum sinense					8	9	10	11	12	1	2	fl 7	
—— *stauntonii*					8	9	10	11	12	1	2	fl 7	
Prunus laurocerasus					8	9	10	11				u # 6	red at first
— *serotina*					8	9						fl u 3	
Rhamnus catharticus					8	9	10					4	
— *frangula*					8	9	10					u 2	red at first
Rhodotypos scandens					8	9	10					fl 5	
Ribes sanguineum					8							fl 5	
Rubus fruticosus					8							cr e u 4	
Sambucus nigra					8	9						e u 5	
Viburnum acerifolium					8	9	10	11				3	
Aralia, all						9	10					fl of 4	
Aronia melanocarpa						9	10	11	12			fl of 4	
Berberis stenophylla						9	10					fl u # 5	
Cornus sanguinea						9						4	
Cotoneaster acutifolius						9	10	11				4	
— *lucidus*						9	10	11				4	
Gaultheria shallon						9	10	11				cr # 5	
Kalopanax pictus						9	10					of 4	
Ligustrum ovalifolium						9	10					# 5	
Phellodendron, all						9	10	11					
Rosa spinosissima						9	10					of 4	
Viburnum lentago						9	10					of fl 2	
Ligustrum amurense							10	11	12	1—4		fl 3	
— *obtusum regelianum*							10	11	12			fl 3	
— *vulgare*							10	11	12			fl 4	

WHITE FRUIT

	4	5	6	7		
Cornus alba			6	7	zone 2	on dark red bark
—— 'Sibirica'			6	7		on scarlet red bark
Morus alba				7	e 4	

Cornus racemosa	.	.	8	.	.	.	.		4
Sorbus koehneana	.	.	8	9	.	.	.		5
— *prattii*	.	.	8	9	.	.	.		5
Symphoricarpos, most	.	.	8	9	10	11	12		u
Gaultheria cuneata	.	.	.9	10	11	.			# 5
— *miqueliana*	.	.	.9	10	11	.			# 5
Pernettya mucronata	.	.	.	10	11	12	1	2	H # 7

LILAC OR PINK FRUITS

Akebia quinata	.	.	.	9	10	.	.	cl 4	lilac
Sorbus vilmorinii	.	.	.	9	10	.	.	5	red turning pink
— *hupehensis*	.	.	.	9	10	.	.	5	bright pink
Callicarpa, all	.	.	.	.	10	11	.	fl	lilac
Pernettya mucronata	.	.	.	.	10	11	.	H # 7	some purple

GRAY FRUIT

Cotinus coggyria	.	7	8	9	.	.	.		5	billowy
Cornus amomum	.	.	8	.	.	.	.		5	gray-blue
Clematis, most	.	.	.	9	10	.	.		fl ss-sh cl	feathery
Myrica pensylvanica	.	.	.	9	10	11	12	1	2	2	waxy layer

OTHER FRUITS

Castanea, all	.	8	9	.	.	.	.	.	.	e	bristly, round
Colutea, all	.	8	9	10	11	.	.	.	.	fl	puffy, bladder-like
Koelreuteria paniculata	.	8	9	10	11	12	1	2	.	fl 5	somewhat as above
Staphylea, all	.	8	9	10	11	12	.	.	.		as above
Catalpa, all	.	.	9	10	11	12	1	2	3	fl	long, stout pod
Liriodendron	.	.	9	10	11	12	1	2	3	fl 4	dry conical pods

DIOECIOUS PLANTS

The following genera are unique in that staminate and pistillate flowers are produced on separate plants. Therefore both male and female plants must be present for fruit production. This is of particular importance with *Ilex* and *Hippophae*.

Acer, many
Ailanthus
Actinidia
Araucaria
Aucuba
Broussonetia
Bacharis
Celastrus
Cephalotaxus
Cercidiphyllum
Chionanthus
Comptonia
Cotinus
Diospyros
Eucommia

Fraxinus
Gingko
Ilex
Gleditsia
Juniperus
Hippophae
Lindera
Maclura
Morus
Myrica
Orixa
Pistacia
Phellodendron
Podocarpus

Populus
Rhus
Ribes
Ruscus
Salix
Schisandra
Shepherdia
Skimmia
Smilax
Taxus
Torreya
Vitis
Zanthoxylon

7. Plants with Poisonous Twigs, Leaves or Fruits

This section is included merely to inform the reader and is by no means a rejection of the listed plants. However, one should be cautious about the use of these plants near schools, playgrounds, home gardens, etc. One should also be aware of those plants poisonous to animals when designing for zoos or near livestock.

Plants	Noxious part	Effect
Juniperus communis	total plant	external: skin irritant internal: inflammatory to stomach, intestines, kidneys; cramping, death
— *sabina*	branch tips	cramping, death
— *virginiana*	needles	rash on susceptible persons
Taxus spp. (the red flesh around the seed is not poisonous!)	branches, needles, seed	internal: stomach, intestinal disturbance to highly poisonous and death: Highly poisonous to livestock
Thuja occidentalis	branches	external: produces rash on susceptible persons
— *orientalis*		internal: as with *Juniperus communis*

Plants	Noxious part	Effect
Andromeda polifolia	total plant, especially new growth	internal: strong narcotic, vomiting, death; for livestock, deadly
Arctostaphylos uva-ursi	leaves and fruit	mild poison, strong diuretic
Cotoneaster types	fruit	contains slight amount of cyanic acid
Cytisus scoparius	total plant	internal: effects nerves, can paralyze
Daphne cneorum	total plant, flowers and fruit	external: causes inflammation on susceptible persons within 2—4 days; consumption of fruit seriously affects stomach, intestines, kidneys; possible death
— *mezereum*		
Euonymus europaeus (among others)	bark, fruit, leaves	internal: vomiting unconciousness, high blood pressure, eventual death
Genista spp.	total plant, seeds	vomiting, loss of breath, fever, rash; deadly to livestock
Hedera helix	total plant	skin irritant of susceptible persons
Kalmia angustifolia	leaves	internal: vomiting, impairs eyesight, shortness of breath; deadly to cattle
— *latifolia*		
Laburnum anagyroides (and others)	leaves, bark, roots, young fruit seed	internal: hyperactivity, cramping, loss of breath, vomiting, possible death
Ledum palustre	branches	internal: vomiting, stimulant at first, later paralysis, dizziness, collapse
Ligustrum vulgare	leaves, bark, fruit	internal: vomiting, diarrhea, colic, eventual death
Lonicera xylosteum	fruit	internal: vomiting, diarrhea, kidney disturbance; eventual death
Lycium halimifolium (and others)	total plant	an atropine although mild; internal: impairs vision, loss of breath, eventual death

Poisonous Plants

Plants	Noxious part	Effect
Maclura pomifera	foliage, fruit	rash from milky sap
Mahonia spp.	foliage, fruit	leaves poisonous, fruit harmless if cooked yet dangerous raw in quantity
Oxydendrum arboreum	leaves	deadly to cattle
Pieris japonica	especially young branches	internal: as with *Andromeda* sp.
Prunus laurocerasus	young branches,	contains cyanic acid, consumption of fruit can cause death
— *serotina*	fruit	
Pyracantha spp.	fruit	contains slight amount of cyanic acid
Rhamnus cathartica	fruit, bark, branches	vomiting, colic, kidney disturbance, collapse;
— *frangula*		deadly to livestock
Rhododendron ponticum	foliage	deadly to cattle
— *catawbiense*		
— *maximum*		
Rhus toxicodendron	foliage	strong, month long skin rash caused by the slightest contact
Rhus glabra	foliage	skin rash on contact by susceptible persons;
— *typhina*		internal; affects stomach, intestines, kidneys, eventual death
Robinia psuedoacacia	seed, fruit, leaves, flowers, bark	internal: colic, cramping, collapse; foliage deadly to horses
Sambucus edulus	fruit and	internal; diarrhea, dizziness, possible death
— *racemosa*	foliage	external: skin rash
Symphoricarpos albus (= *S. racemosus*)	fruit	internal: upset stomach when eaten in large amounts
Viburnum spp.	bark, leaves, fruit	consumption of large quantities cause inflammation of stomach, intestines, nerve damage, possible death
— *lantana*		
— *opulus*		
Wisteria sinensis	branches	upset stomach, diarrhea, collapse

8. Conditional Plants

The following list contains plants with particular problems which should be considered before their use.

Plants	Problem	Caution when planting in
Berberis vulgaris (and nearly all) deciduous *Berberis*)	alternate host for rust of grain	agricultural areas, within 300 m of a grain field
Crataegus monogyna — *oxycantha* (and others)	breeding place for fruit tree pests	orchard areas
Juniperus sabina — *communis* — *virginiana*	intermediate host for Cedar — Apple Rust	avoid planting near orchards or other Rosaceous species
Lonicera tatarica — *xylosteum*	breeding place of of cherry fruit fly	avoid planting near cherries
Mahoberberis var.	many alternate hosts of wheat rust	avoid in wheat producing areas
Prunus padus	breeds an aphid pest of oats	avoid in agricultural areas
Prunus spinosa	breeding place for many fruit tree pests and an aphid on hops	avoid in orchard areas or plantings of hops
Rhamnus catharticus	alternate host of Black Stem Rust	avoid strictly from grain producing areas
Viburnum opulus	breeding place of black aphid, pest of beets and beans	avoid vegetable garden areas
Ribes, most	alternate host of white pine blister rust	avoid planting all except; R. alpinum (males)

II. THE USES OF THE PLANTS

1. Plants for Certain Soil Types

a. Plants for Moist to Wet Soils

Most tolerate moist soils; w = likes wet soil

BROADLEAVES

Acer negundo, zone 2
— *rubrum,* 3 of fl
— *saccharinum,* 3
Alnus spp.
Amelanchier spp. fl fr
Andromeda polifolia, 2 # w
Aronia arbutifolia, 4 dr
Betula nigra, 4 of
— *pubescens,* 2 w
Calluna vulgaris, 4 # fl
Celtis occidentalis, 2
Calycanthus floridus, 4 fl
Cephalanthus occidentalis, 4 w fl
Cercidiphyllum japonicum, 4 of
Chamaedaphne calyculata, 3 # fl
Clethra alnifolia, 3 fl F
Comptonia peregrina, 2 of
Cornus alba, 2 of fr
Cornus amomum, zone 5 fl fr
— *sanguinea,* 4 fl fr
— *stolonifera,* 2 fl fr
Daphne mezereum, 4 fl
Erica tetralix, 3 # fl
Dirca palustris, 4 w fl
Enkianthus campanulatus, 4 of fl
Euonymus europaeus, 3 fr
Fraxinus excelsior, 3
Gaultheria shallon, 5 # of fl fr
Hippophae rhamnoides, 3 of fr
Hydrangea spp. fl
Ilex glabra, 3 # of
— *verticillata,* 3 of fr
Itea virginica, 5 fl
Kalmia latifolia, 4 # fl
Ledum palustre, 2 # w fl
— *groenlandicum,* 2 # w fl

Leucothoe fontanesiana, zone 4 # fl
Liquidambar styraciflua, 5 of
Liriodendron tulipifera, 4 of
Lindera benzoin, 4
Lonicera coerulea, 6 fr
Magnolia virginiana, 5 fl F
Myrica spp.
Nyssa silvatica, 4 of
Parrotia persica, 5 of fl
Populus alba, 3 of
— *canescens,* 4
— *tremula,* 2
Pterocarya fraxinifolia, 5 of fr
Quercus bicolor, 3 of
— *palustris,* 4 of
Rhamnus frangula, 2 fr
Rhododendron calendulaceum, zone 5 fl
— *canadensis,* 2 fl
— *vaseyi,* 4 fl
Rhododendron viscosum, zone 3 fl
Rosa palustris, 4 fl fr
— *rugosa,* 2 fl fr
Rubus odoratus, 3 fl
Salix spp.
Sambucus nigra, 5 fl fr
— *canadensis,* 3 fl fr
Spirea menziesii, 6 fl
— *salicifolia,* 6 fl
Vaccinium corymbosum, 3 fr
— *macrocarpum,* 3 # fr
— *uliginosum,* 3 w fr
Viburnum alnifolium, 3 of fl
— *cassinoides,* 2 of fl
— *dentatum,* 2 fl fr
— *opulus,* 3 fl fr
— *trilobum,* 2 fl fr
Zenobia pulverulenta, 5 fl

CONIFERS

Abies spp. #
Chamaecyparis pisifera, 3 #
Casuarina spp. 8
Juniperus communis montana, 2 #
Larix laricina, 2 w
Libocedrus decurrens, 5
Pinus mugo uncinata, 2 #
— *strobus*, 3 #
Taxodium distichum, 4 w

Metasequoia glyptostroboides, 5
Picea abies, 5 #
— *glauca*, 2 # w
— *jezoensis*, 4 #
— *mariana*, 2 # w
— *sitchensis*, 6 # w
Taxus canadensis, 2 #
Thuja occidentalis, 2 # w

(Tolerates standing water up to one week)

BROADLEAVES

Acer platanoides, zone 3
'— — 'Schwedleri' etc.
— *japonicum* 'Filicifolium', 5
Carpinus betulus, 4
Catalpa bignonoides, 4
Cornus alba, 2
Corylus avellana, 3
Euonymus europaeus, 3
— *fortunei*, 5 #
Hibiscus syriacus, 5
Hypericum patulum, 6

Lonicera caprifolium, 4
— *purpusii*, 4
Philadelphus grandiflorus, 4
Populus alba, 3
— — 'Pyramidalis'
— *canadensis* 'Robusta', 4
Prunus padus, 3
— *virginiana*, 2
Quercus robur, 5
Sophora japonica, 4
Viburnum plicatum, 4

CONIFERS

Metasequoia glyptostroboides, 5 of   *Taxodium distichum*, 4 of

(Tolerates longer periods of standing water)

BROADLEAVES

Acer pseudoplatanus, 5
— *palmatum*, 5
Broussonetia papyrifera, 6
Buddleia alternifolia, 5
Fraxinus excelsior, zone 3
Syringa vulgaris, 3
  (and var.)
Ulmus carpinifolia, 4
Viburnum burkwoodii, 5 #
— *rhytidophyllum*, 5 #

Buddleia davidii, 5
Buxus sempervirens, 5
Deutzia, all
Forsythia, all
Hydrangea arborescens, 4
— *macrophylla*, 5
Ilex aquifolium, 5 #
Prunus laurocerasus, 6
Sambucus nigra, 5

Sandy Soil

b. Plants for Sandy, Dry to Sterile Soil

("S" denotes the best types)

BROADLEAVES

Acanthopanax sieboldianus, 4
Acer ginnala, 2 of
— *negundo*, 2
Ailanthus altissima, 4 S
Albizzia julibrissin, 7 fl
Alnus glutinosa, 3 S
— *incana*, 2 S
Amelanchier spp. fl fr
Amorpha canescens, 2 S fl of
Aralia elata, 3 of fl fr
Arctostaphylos uva-ursi, 2 # S
Artemesia spp. S
Berberis (deciduous types)
Betula davurica, 4 S
— *pendula*, 2 S
— *populifolia*, 3 S
Broussonetia papyrifera, 6 of fr
Caragana arborescens, 2 S
Ceanothus americanus, 4 S fl
Celtis australis, 6
Chaenomeles spp. fl fr
Colutea arborescens, 5 S fl fr
Comptonia peregrina, 2 of
Cornus sanguinea, 4 of fl fr
— *racemosa*, 4 fl fr
Cotinus coggygria, 5 S of fl fr
Cytisus scoparius, S fl
Diervilla sessilifolia, 4 fl
Eleagnus angustifolia, 2 S of fr
Elsholtzia stauntonii, 4 fl
Eucalyptus spp.
Euonymus japonica, 8 # of
Fraxinus velutina, 5 of
Gleditsia triacanthos, 4 of
Garrya spp. # fl
Genista spp. fl
Hamamelis virginiana, zone 4 fl
Hebe spp. # fl
Helianthemum, all su fl
Hippophae rhamnoides, 3 of fr fl
Hypericum calycinum, 6 # of fr
Indigofera gerardiana, 5 fl
Koelreuteria paniculata, 5 fl
Kolkwitzia amabilis, 4 fl

Laburnum spp. fl
Lavandula, all # of fl
Lespedeza bicolor, 4 fl
— *thunbergii*, 4 fl
Buddleia alternifolia, 5 fl
Lycium, all fr
Melia azedarach, 7 of fl fr F
Maclura pomifera, F
Nerium oleander, 7 fl of #
Olea europaea, 9 fr fl F
Perovskia, all of fl
Physocarpus, spp.
Pittosporum app. # of fl F
Populus alba, 3 of
Potentilla spp. fl
Prunus maritima, 3 fl
— *serotina*, 3 fl fr
— *spinosa*, 4 fl fr e
Rhamnus frangula, 2 fr
Rhus typhina, 5 of fl fr
Ribies alpinum, 2
Robinia hispida, 5 fl
— *psuedoacacia*, 3 fl
Rosa carolina, 4 fl fr
— *rubiginosa*, 5 fl fr
— *rugosa*, 2 fl fr
Rubus spectabilis, 5 su fl
Rosmarinus officinalis, 6 fl #
Ruscus aculeatus, 7 # fr of
Santolina, all # of
Sassafras albidum, 4 of
Shepherdia spp. of fr
Sophora japonica, 4 of fl fr
Sorbus aucuparia, 2 of fl fr
Spartium junceum, 7 fl
Symphoricarpos, all fr
Tamarix, all fl
Teucrium chamaedrys, 5 of
Ulex europaeus, 6 fl
Ulmus pumila, 4
Viburnum lantana, zone 3 of su-sh fl
— *lentago*, 2 of fl fr
Yucca filamentosa, 4 # of fl

EVERGREEN

Abies cephalonica, 5
— *concolor*, 4
— *homolepsis*, 4
Casuarina spp.
Cupressus macrocarpa
Ephedra, most
Juniperus communis, 2
— *conferta*, 5
— *virginiana*, 2
— *horizontalis*, 3

Picea omorika, 4
— *pungens*, 2
Pinus banksiana, 2
— *contorta*, 7
— *mugo*, 2
— *nigra austriaca*, 4
— *ponderosa*, 5
— *rigida*, 4
— *silvestris*, 2
— *virginiana*, 4

c. Plants for Heavy Clay Soil

Soil improvement by addition of compost or peat and mulch recommended in most cases.

Acer platanoides, zone 3
Betula pendula, 2 of fl
Chaenomeles speciosa, 4 fl fr
Clematis, common types fl
Colutea arborescens, 5 fl fr
Cornus mas, 4 su-sh fl fr of
Corylus avellana, 3 su-sh of fl fr e
Cotinus coggygria, 5 of fl fr
Cytisus purpureus, 5 fl
— *scoparius*, 5 fl
Deutzia gracilis, 4 fl
— *scabra*, 5 fl
Euonymus spp. su-sh of
Hamamelis virginiana, 4 of fl
Hypericum calycinum, zone 6 #
  su-sh # of fl
Ilex aquifolium, 5 # su-sh of fr
Jasminum nudiflorum, 5 fl

Kerria japonica, 4 fl
Laburnum types fl
Magnolia kobus, 5 fl
Malus spp. fl
Philadelphus types fl
Prunus, most fl
Pyrus spp. fl.
Rhus glabra, 2 of fl fr
Ribes sanguineum, f fl
Robinia pseudoacacia, 3 of fl
Sambucus racemosa, 4 sh fl fr
Spartium junceum, 7 fl
Tamarix gallica, 6 fl
Viburnum lantana, 3 su-sh of fl fr
— *opulus*, 3 su-sh fl fr
Weigela spp. fl
Yucca filamentosa, 4 # su of fl

d. Plants for Gravel Slopes

SUNNY OR SOUTH SLOPES

Amelanchier ovalis, zone 4 of fl fr
Betula pendula, 2
Berberis thunbergii, 4 of fl fr
Caragana spp. fl
Clematis vitalba, 4 fl
Cornus alba, 2 fl fr
Coronilla emerus, 4 fl
Cotoneaster apiculata, 4 dr
Cytisus nigricans, 5 fl
— *scoparius*, 5 fl
Eleagnus angustifolia, 2 of fr
Erica carnea, 5 # fl
— *cinerea*, 5 # fl (acid soil)
— *vagans*, 5 # fl (acid soil)
Euonymus fortunei, 5 # of
Genista sagittalis, 6 of fl
— *tinctoria*, 2 fl
Hebe spp. # of
Helianthemum spp. # fl
Juniperus spp. #
Kerria japonica, 4 fl

Ligustrum vulgare, 4
Lycium, all fr
Physocarpus spp.
Pinus mugo, 2 # su
Potentilla spp. fl
Prunus pumila, 4 fl
— *spinosa*, 4 fl fr e
— *tenella*, 4 fl
Rhus spp. of fl fr
ribes alpinum, 2 fr
Robinia psuedoacacia, 3 fl
Rosa wichuriana, zone 5 fl
— *rugosa*, 2 fl fr
Rubus fruticosa, 4 fr e
Sambucus nigra, 5 fl fr e
Spartium junceum, 7 fl
Spirea x billardi, 4 fl
— *douglasii*, 4 fl
— *salicifolia*, 6 fl
Xanthorrhiza simplicissima, 4 of

SHADED OR NORTH SLOPES

Betula pubescens, zone 2
— *pendula*, 2
Clematis vitalba, 4 fl
Comptonia peregrina, 2 of
Cornus alba, 2 fl fr
— *sanguinea*, 4 fl fr
Cotoneaster dammeri, 5 # fl fr
Diervilla sessilifolia, 4 fl
Forsythia 'Arnold's Dwarf', 5
— *suspensa*, 5 fl
Gaultheria procumbens, 3 # of fl fr e
— *shallon*, 5 # fl fr
Leucothoe fontanesiana, 4 4 of fl
— *vulgare*, 4
— — 'Atrovirens' of
Lonicera xylosteum 'Claveyi', 4 fl

Prunus serotina, 3 of fl fr
— *virginiana*, 2 fl fr
Rhododendron (small leaved types)
    # fl see list p. 42
Rhus glabra, 2 of fr
— *aromatica*, 3 of fr
— *typhina*, 5 of fr
Ribes alpinum, 2 fr
Rubus odoratus, 4 fl
Spirea douglasii, 4 fl
— *salicifolia*, 6 fl
Syringa vulgaris, 3 fl
— *salicifolia*, 6 fl
Vaccinium vitis-idaea, 2 # fr e
Xanthorrhiza simplicissima, 4 of

e. Plants for Alkaline Soil

Those plants designated by the symbol 'A' will tolerate alkaline soil, but prefer neutral soil.

BROADLEAVES

Acer campestre, zone 5 of
Ailanthus altissima, 4 of
Alnus incana, 2 of
Berberis, all except
   B. thunbergii, of fr
Buddleia davidii types, 5 fl
Buxus sempervirens, 5 # of
Carpinus betulus, 4 of
Catalpa bignonioides, 4 of fl
Cercis siliquastrum, 6 fl
Chaenomeles spp. fl fr
Cladrastis spp. of fl
Clematis spp. fl fr
Colutea spp. fl fr
Cornus mas, 4 fl fr
— sanguinea, 4 fl fr
Corylus spp. A fl fr e
Cotinus spp. of fl fr
Cotoneaster spp. of fl fr
Crataegus spp. of fl fr
Cytisus purpureus, 5 fl
Dryas octopetala, 4 # of fl fr
Erica carnea, 5 # fl
Euonymus europaeus, 3 A fr
Exochorda spp. fl
Fagus silvatica, 4 of
Forsythia spp. A fl
Fraxinus excelsior, 3
— ornus, 5
Fuchsia gracilis, 7 A fl
Genista radiata, 6 A fl
Halimodendron halodendron, 2 of fl
Hebe, all #
Helianthemum, fl #
Hippophae rhamnoides, 3 of fr
Ilex aquifolium, 5 # of fr
Jasminum nudiflorum, 5 fl
Kerria japonica, 4 fl
Koelruteria spp. of fl fr

Laburnum spp. fl
Lavandula angustifolia, 6 # of fl
Lonicera spp. fl fr
Ligustrum vulgare, 4 fr
Malus spp. fl fr e
Paulownia spp. A of fl
Philadelphus spp. fl
Physocarpus spp. fl
Populus spp. of
Prunus, most of fl fr
Pyracantha spp. # fl fr
Pyrus spp. of fl fr
Quercus cerris, 6 of
— frainetto, 5 of
— robur, 5 of
Rhamnus catharticus, **4 fr**
Rhododendron hirsutum, 4 # fl
Rhus typhina, 5 of fl fr
Ribes alpinum, 2 of fr
— sanguineum, 5 fl
Robinia spp. fl
Rosa spp. fl fr
Rosmarinus officinalis, zone 6 # of fl
Salix spp. of fl
Sambucus nigra, 5 fl fr
Santolina spp. #
Sophora japonica, 4 of fl
Sorbus aria, 5 of fl fr
Spartium junceum, 7 fl
Spirea, most fl
Staphylea spp. of fl fr
Symphoricarpos spp. fr
Syringa vulgaris, 3 fl
Teucrium chamaedrys, 5 # of
Ulex europaeus, 6 A fl
Viburnum lantana, 3 A of fl fr
— opulus, 3 A fl fr
Weigela spp. fl

EVERGREENS

Cedrus atlantica 'Glauca' zone 6 # of
Juniperus communis, 2 #
— sabina, 4 #
Picea abies, 5 #

Pinus leucodermis, 5 #
— mugo, 2 A #
— nigra, 4 #
Taxus baccata, 5 # A

f. Plants for Acid Soil

BROADLEAVES

Acer palmatum, zone 5 of
— *rubrum*, 3 of fl
Amelanchier laevis, 4 fl fr
Andromeda polifolia, 2 # fl
Arbutus unedo, 8 fl fr
(Azaleas) fl
Berberis thunbergii, 4 of fl fr
Betula, most
Callicarpa spp. fl fr.
Calluna spp. # fl.
Camellia spp. # of fl
Castanea spp. of fl fr e
Clethra alnifolia, 3 fl
Cornus florida, 4 of fl fr
— *kousa*, 4 of fl fr
— *stolonifera*, 2 fl fr
Cotoneaster, # of fl fr
(evergreen types)
Cyrilla racemiflora, 5 # fl
Cytisus scoparius, 5 fl
Daboecia cantabrica, 5 # fl
Empetrum spp. # of fr
Enkianthus spp. of fl
Erica, all (except *E. carnea*) # fl
Epigea repens, 2 # ss fl F
Fothergilla, all of fl
Gaultheria, all # fl fr
Genista sagittalis, 6 fl
— *tinctoria*, 2 fl
Halesia carolina, 4 of fl fr
Hamamelis, all of fl
Hydrangea, all fl
Ilex, all # of fr
Illicium floridanum, 7 # of fl
Itea virginica, 5 of fl F

Kalmia spp. # fl of
Kalmiopsis leachiana, 6 fl
Ledum groenlandicum, 2 # of fl
Leiophyllum buxifolium, 5 # of fl
Leucothoe fontanesiana, 4 # of fl
Loiseleuria procumbens, 2 # of fl
Lonicera coerulea, 6 of fr
Magnolia, all fl
Parrotia persica, 5 of fl
Pernettya, all # of fr
Pieris floribunda, 4 # S fl
— *japonica*, 5 # H fl of
Poncirus trifoliata, 6 fl fr
Populus canescens, zone 4 of
— *tremula*, 2 of
Potentilla fruticosa, 2 fl
Quercus petraea, 4 of
— *palustris*, 4 of
Rhododendron, most # fl of
Rosa rugosa, 2 fl fr
Sambucus racemosa, 4 fl fr
Skimmia spp. # of fl fr
Stranvaesia spp. # of fr
Ulex europaeus, 6 fl
Vaccinium spp. of fr.
Viburnum burkwoodii, 5 # fl F
— *alnifolia*, 3 of fl fr
— *carlesi*, 4 fl F
— *farreri*, 5 fl
— *nudum*, 6 of fl fr
Weigela 'Eva Rathke', 5 fl
— *middendorffiana*, 4 fl
Xanthorhiza simplicissima, 4 of
Zenobia pulverulenta, 5 ss fl

CONIFEROUS

Abies procera 'Glauca', 5 #
— *veitchii*, 3 #
Juniperus chinensis 'Pfitzeriana, 4 #

Picea sitchensis, 6 #
Pinus cembra, 4 #
— *mugo*, 2 #

g. Plants for the Sea Coast

Those noted with "Du" will tolerate dune planting.

Acer platanoides, zone 3 of fl
— *pseudoplatanus*, 5 of
Aesculus hippocastanum, 3 of fl
Ailanthus altissima, 4 of
Amelanchier canadensis, 4 fl fr
Betula pendula, 2
Calluna vulgaris, 4 # Du fl
Caragana arborescens, 2 fl
Celastrus spp. fr
Comptonia peregrina, 2 of
Cornus sanguinea, 2 fl fr
Crataegus crus-galli, 4 fl fr
— *monogyna*, 4 fl fr
— *oxycantha*, 4 fl fr
Cytisus scoparius, 5 Du fl
Eleagnus angustifolia, 2 Du of
Empetrum nigrum, 2 # Du of
Fraxinus velutina, 5
Halimodendron halodendron, zone 2 of fl
Hibiscus syriacus, 5 fl
Hippophae rhamnoides, 3 Du of fr 3
Hydrangea macrophylla, 5 fl
Ilex aquifolium, 5 # of fr
— *glabra*, 3 # of
— *opaca*, 5 # of fr
Laburnum anagyroides, 5 fl
Lavendula spp. fl
Lonicera japonica 'Halliana, 4 # fl F
— *nitida*, 7 # of
— *tatarica*, 3 fl
Lycium spp. of fr
Mahonia aquifolium, 5 # fl fr of
Magnolia grandiflora, 7 # o fl
Morus alba, 4
Myrica spp. # fr
Nyssa sylvatica, 4 of
Olea europaea, 6 of fl F

Populus alba, 3 Du of
— *tremula*, 2 of
Prunus maritima, 3 fl
— *serotina*, 3 Du fl fr
— *spinosa*, 4 Du fl fr e
Potentilla spp. fl
Quercus alba, 4 of
Quercus ilex, zone 7 # of
— *marilandica*, 6 of
— *robur*, 5 Du of
— *virginiana* 7 # of
Rhamnus catharticus, 4 fr
Rhus spp. of fl fr
Robinia pseudoacacia, 3 Du fl
Rosa canina, 3 fl fr e
— *rubiginosa*, 5 of fl fr e
— *rugosa*, 2 fl fr e
— *pimpinellifolia*, 5 Du fl fr
— *virginiana*, 3 fl
— *wichuriana*, 5 fl
Salix alba, 2 Du
— *caprea*, 4 fl
— *purpurea*, 3 Du of
— *repens*, 4 Du of
Sambucus nigra, 5 Du fl fr e
— *canadensis*, 3 fl fr 3
Sorbus aria, 5 of fl fr
— *aucuparia*, 2 of fl fr
Tamarix, all fl
Tilia cordata, 3 Du fl F
— *euchlora*, 5 fl F
Ulex europaeus, 6 Du fl
Ulmus parviflora, 5 of
Ulmus pumila, zone 4
Viburnum dentatum, 2 fl fr
Viburnum opulus, 3 Du fl fr
— *tinus*, 7 # of fl fr

Frost Free Sea Coasts

ADDITIONAL PLANTS FOR FROST FREE SEA COASTS

Escallonia, all # of fl
Eucalyptus spp. of
Griselinia littoralis, zone 9 # of
Nerium oleander, 8 # fl of
Pittosporum tobira, 8 # fl of
Olearia forsteri, 9 of fl
— *haastii*, 8 # of fl
— *ilicifolia*, 9 # of fl
— *macrodonta*, 9 # of fl

Olearia scilloniensis, 9 # of fl
— *semidentata*, 9 # of fl
— *solanderi*, 9 # of fl
— *traversii*, 9 # of fl
Senecio eleagnifolius, 9 # of fl
— *laxifolius*, 9 # o fl
— *morrowii*, 9 # of fl
— *rotundifolius*, 9 # of fl

CONIFERS

Araucaria spp. 3 of
Casuarina spp. #
Cupressus macrocarpa, 7 #
Cryptomeria japonica, 5 #
Juniperus chinensis, 4 #
— *communis*, 2 #
— *conferta*, 5 #
— *horizontalis*, 3 #
— *virginiana*, 2 #
Picea asperata, 5 #
— *pungens*, 2 #

Picea sitchensis, zone 6 # Du
Pinus mugo, 2 # du
— *nigra*, 4 # Du
— *pinaster*, 7 # Du
— *rigida*, 4 #
— *radiata*, 7 #
— *silvestris*, 2 # Du
— *thunbergii*, 5 # Du
Thuja occidentalis, 2 #
— *orientalis*, 6 #

2. Shade Loving and Shade Tolerant Plants

(u = useful in understory planting)

DECIDUOUS

Acanthopanax sieboldianus, zone 4 of fr
Acer campestre, 5 of
— *circinatum*, 5 of
— *pensylvanicum*, 3 of
— *spicatum*, 2 of
Alnus spp. of
Amelanchier spp. of fl fr
Aralia elata, 3 u of fl
Aronia, all of fl fr
Berberis mentorensis, 5 uf of
— *thunbergii*, 4 of fl fr
Carpinus betulus, 4 u
Celastrus, all fr
Cercis canadensis, 4 fl of
Clematis, all fl
Clethra alnifolia, 3 cu fl F
Colutea arborescens, 5 fl fr
Comptonia peregrina, 2 u of
Cornus alba, 2 u fl fr
— *amomum*, 5 u fl fr
— *florida*, 5 u fl
— *mas*, 4 u fl fr
— *stolonifera*, 2 u fl fr
Corylopsis, all u fl
Corylus spp. fr e
Cotoneaster divaricatus, 5 u fl fr
— *watereri*, 6 fl fr
— — 'Pendulus' fl fr
— — 'Cornubia' fl fr
Crataegus monogyna, 4 u fl fr
Daphne mezereum, 4 u fl fr
Diervilla sessilifolia, 4 u of fl
Enkianthus campanulatus, 4 u of fl
Euonymus europaeus, 3 u fr
Fagus silvatica, 4 of
Fothergilla, all u of fl
Hamamelis, all u of fl
Hydrangea anomala petiolaris, zone 4, u fl
— *aspera*, 7 of fl
— — *sargentiana*, of fl
— *macrophylla*, 5 fl
— *quercifolia*, 5 of fl

Kerria japonica, 4 u fl
Ligustrum vulgare, 4 u of
Lindera benzoin, 4
Lonicera caprifolium, 4 fl fr
Lonicera coerulea, zone 6 u fr
— *xylosteum*, 4 u fr
Parthenocissus quinquefolia, zone 3 of
Philadelphus spp. fl
Populus canescens, 4 of
— *tremula*, 2 of
Prunus avium, 3 fl fr 3
— *padus*, 3 u fl fr
— *serotina*, 3 u fl fr
— *virginiana*, 2 u fl fr
— *subhirtella*, 5 fl
Rhamnus catharticus, 4 u fr
— *frangula*, 2 u fr
Rhododendron spp. fl
Rhodotypos scandens, 5 u fl fr
Ribes alpinum, 2 u fr
— *odoratum*, 4 fl F fr
— *sanguineum*, 5 u fl
Rubus odoratus, 3 u of fl
Rubus spectabilis, 5 u of fl
Salix caprea, 4 fl
Sambucus nigra, 5 u fl fr 3
— *racemosa*, 4 u fr
Sorbus aucuparia, 2 of fl fr
Stachyurus praecox, 6 u fl
Stephanandra incisa, 5 of
Styrax spp. fl
Symphoricarpos, all u fr
Viburnum dentatum, 2 u fl fr
— *lantana*, 3 u of fl fr
— *lentago*, 2 of fl fr
— *opulus*, 3 u fl fr
— *plicatum*, 4 fl fr
— *prunifolium*, 3 of fl fr
— *sieboldii*, 4 of fl fr
Zenobia pulverulenta, 5 u fl
Xanthorhiza simplicissima,, 4 of

Shade Tolerance

BROADLEAF EVERGREENS
(all #)

Abelia grandiflora, 5 of fl
Andromeda polifolia, zone 2 of fl
Aucuba japonica, 7 of fr
Arundinaria spp.
Berberis (evergreen types)
— *gagnepainii lancifolia*, 5 u of
— *julianae*, 5 u of fl fr
— *verruculosa*, 5 u of fl
Buxus, all u of
Camellia japonica, 7 fl
Cotoneaster dammeri, 5 fl fr
— *salicifolius floccosus*, 6 u of fl
— — 'Parkteppich', u fl fr
Euonymus fortunei, 5 u of
Gaultheria procumbens, 3 of fr
Gaultheria shallon, zone 5 u of fr
Hedera, all of
Hypericum calycinum, 6 fl
Ilex, all of fr
Kalmia, all uf of fl
Leucothoe fontanesiana, 4 u of fl
Ligustrum ovalifolium, 5 uf of
Lonicera nitida 'Elegant',
    zone 7 u of
— *pileata*, 5 of

Magnolia virginiana, 5 of fl F
Mahonia, all u of fl fr
Myrica spp. fr
Nandina domestica, of fl
Osmanthus, all u of
Pachysandra terminalis, 5 of fl
Paxistima canbyi, 5 of fl fr
Photinia spp. of fl fr
Pieris floribunda, 4 fl
— *japonica*, 5 of fl
— *taiwanensis*, 7 of fl
Pittosporum tobira, 8 of fl
Prunus laurocerasus, all u of
Pyracantha, all u fr
Rhododendron, most fl
Sarcococca, allu of
Skimmia japonica, 7 of fr
— *reevesiana* 'Rubella', 7 fl
Stranvaesia davidiana, 6 u fr
Vaccinium spp. of fr e
Viburnum burkwoodii, 5 u of fl F
— *rhytidophyllum*, 5 of fl fr
— *tinus*, 7 u of fl fr
Vinca minor, 4 of fl

CONIFERS

Chamaecyparis, all
Juniperus chinensis, zone 4
— — 'Pfitzeriana'
— *horizontalis*, 3
— *sabina*, 4
Picea abies, 5

Picea orientalis, 4
Taxus spp.
Thuja spp.
Thujopsis dolabrata, 6
Tsuga spp.
— *heterophylla*, 1, 6

3. Recommended Specimen Plants

BROADLEAVES

Trees

Acer capillipes	of fr	zone 6	green bark, striped white
— *griseum*	of	5	cinnamon brown bark
— *nikoense*	of fr	5	good red fall color
— *palmatum*	*of*	5	delicate foliage
— *pensylvanicum*	of	3	green, white striped bark
Aesculus carnea 'Brioti'	of fl	3	deep red flowers
Albizzia julibrissin	of fl	7	feather foliage
Arbutus menziesii	of fl fr	7	smooth red trunk
Betula albosinensis	of	5	orange-red bark
— *nigra*	of	4	flaking, cream bark
— *papyrifera*	of	2	white bark
— *populifolia*	of	3	white bark
— *pendula*	of	2	bark white, dark markings
— — 'Gracilis'	of		broadly weeping
— — 'Tristis'	of wg		narrowly weeping
Catalpa bignonioides	fl	4	white flowers, large leaves
Cercis spp.	of fl		good foliage, wide canopy
Cladrastis lutea	of fl	3	white flowers
Cornus nutallii	of fl	7	large flowering tree
Davidia involucrata *vilmoriniana*	of fl	5	white flowers
Fagus silvatica 'Asplenifolia'	of	4	delicate foliage
— — 'Riversii'	of		dark purple foliage
Gleditsia 'Sunburst'	of	4	yellow foliage
Franklinia alatamaha	of fl	5	white flowers
Eleagnus angustifolia	of	2	silvery foliage
Kalopanax pictus	of	4	good foliage, shade tree
Koelreuteria paniculata	of fl	5	yellow summer flowers
Liquidambar styraciflua	of	5	red fall foliage
Liriodendron tulipifera	of	4	attractive foliage
Phellodendron amurense	of	3	wide, open shade tree
Photinia serrulata	of fl fr	7	white flowers
Platanus acerifolia	of	5	large shade tree
Poncirus trifoliata	of fl F	6	white, fragrant flowers
Populus alba	of	3	silvery foliage
— *koreana*	of	4	large leaves
— *lasiocarpa*	of	5	very large leaves
— *wilsonii*	of	5	large leaves
Prunus avium 'Plena'	fl	3	full, white flowers
— *padus* 'Watereri'	fl	3	long flower clusters
— *sargentii*	fl	4	pink flowers, early
— *serrulata*	fl	5	(Japanese flowering cherries)
— — 'Hokusai'	fl		bright pink, semi-double
— — 'Jonioi'	fl F		white, simple
— — 'Kansan'	fl		pink, full

Specimen Plants

— — 'Shirofugen'	fl		white, simple, early
— — 'Tai-haku'	fl		white, very large flower
— — 'Ukon'	fl		cream, simple
— yedoense	fl	zone 5	white-pink, very early
Pterocarya fraxinifolia	of fr	5	large leaves
Quercus frainetto	of	5	lacy leaves
— macranthera	of	5	good foliage
— petraea	of	4	very straight growing
— robur	of	5	clean attractive foliage
— — 'Fastigiata'	of		pyramidal habit
Robinia psuedoacacia 'Semperflorens'	of fl	3	flowers June and Sept.
— — 'Tortuosa'	of fl		interesting branch habit
Salix alba 'Tristis'	of wg	2	needs room to grow
Sophora japonica	of fl	4	late summer flowers
Sorbus aucuparia	of fl fr	2	good fruit effect
— domestica	of fl fr	5	pear shaped fruit
— intermedia	of fl fr	5	good foliage, red fruit
— latifolia	of fl fr	4	large yellowish fruit
— sargentiana	e of fl fr	6	large leaves, fall color
Stewartia spp.	fl		white flowers
Tilia cordata	of fl F	3	good shade tree
— petiolaris	of fl F	5	branches pendulous
— platyphylla	of fl F	3	large leaves
— tomentosa	of fl F	4	whitish under-leaf

Tall shrubs, 5m and over

Acer carpinifolium	of	5	attractive foliage
— negundo 'Odessanum'	of	2	yellow foliage
— — 'Variegatum'	of		white edged leaves
Alnus glutinosa 'Imperialis'	of	3	cutleaf foliage
— incana 'Aurea'	of	2	yellow twigs and leaves
Amelanchier laevis	of fl fr	4	good foliage, flower & fruit
Arbutus unedo	of fl fr	8	good bark, flowers & fruit
Cornus florida	of fl	4	white flowers
— kousa	of fl fr e	5	longer lasting flower
— mas	fl fr	4	yellow flowers, early
— officinalis	fl	4	as above
Crataegus spp.			very hardy, good for wildlife
Halesia carolina	fl fr	4	white flower 'bells'
— monticola	fl fr	5	as above
Hamamelis spp.	of fl		small yellow flowers in winter
Ilex aquifolium	of fr #	5	red fruit
— — 'J.C. van Tol'	of fr #		abundant fruit
— — 'Pyramidalis'	of fr #		columnar plant
Laburnum watereri 'Vossii'	fl	5	long yellow flower panicles
Magnolia kobus	fl	5	white flowers
— soulangiana	fl	5	pink flowers
— — 'Lennei'	fl		purplish flower
— virginiana	of fl F #	5	fragrant white flower

Malus spp. see list p. 48	fl fr		
Nothofagus antarctica	of	zone 7	fine foliage
Oxydendrum arboreum	of fl	5	white summer flowers
Parrotia persica	of fl	5	mottled bark
Prunus cerasifera 'Pissardii'	of	3	purple foliage
— — 'Accolade'	fl		pink flower, good habit
— — 'Pandora'	fl		upright, pink flower
— *subhirtella* 'Autumnalis'	fl	5	white flower in fall!
— — 'Pendula'	wg fl		pink, weeping
Pterostyrax hispida	of fl	5	white panicles
Rhus glabra	of fl fr	2	twigs bluish white
— *typhina*	of fl fr	5	twigs densely pubescent
Salix caprea mas	fl	4	(pussy willow)
— *acutifolia* 'Pendulifolia'	of fl	4	good bark
Sambucus canadensis			
'Maxima'	of fl fr	3	large flower cluster
Sophora japonica 'Pendula'	of fl	4	weeping habit
Styrax japonica	fl	5	white flowers
— *obassia*	of fl fr	5	white flower panicles

Medium height shrubs, 2—3m

Aralia elata	of fl	3	multistem, large leaves
Arundinaria murielae	of #	6	bamboo, yellowish canes
Camellia japonica	of fl #	7	white to red flowers
Chionanthus virginica		4	white flowers
Choisya ternata	of fl F #	7	fragrant white flower
Corylus avellana 'Contorta'		3	corkscrew twigs
— *maxima* 'Purpurea'	of	4	purple foliage
Cotinus coggygria	fl fr	5	interesting fruit effect
— — 'Rubrifolia'	of fl fr		as above, purple leaves
Cotoneaster watereri	of fl fr	6	red fruit
— *salicifolia floccosa*	of fr #	6	red fruit
Decaisnea fargesii	of fr	6	blue pod fruit
Enkianthus campanulatus	of fl	4	red-yellow flowers
Forsythia intermedia			
'Spectabilis'	fl	5	abundant yellow flowers
Fothergilla spp.	fl		white spike flowers
Hibiscus syriacus	fl	5	lilac, red, white, blue
Kalmia latifolia	of fl # 4		waxy white flowers
Kolkwitzia amabilis	fl	4	light pink flower
Lonicera maackii	of fl fr	2	white flower, red fruit
Magnolia kobus 'Loebneri'	fl	5	white, hardy
— *sieboldii*	of fl fr	5	white in summer
— *stellata*	fl	5	white, very hardy
Mahonia aquifolium'	of fl fr #	5	yellow flower
Philadelphus 'Virginal'	fl F	5	white full, double
Pieris japonica	of fl #	5	white, good foliage
Prunus triloba	fl	5	pink, full flowers
Pyracantha 'Orange Glow'	of fr #	6	good fruit effect
Rhododendron spp.	of fl #		see list p. 46

Age & Height

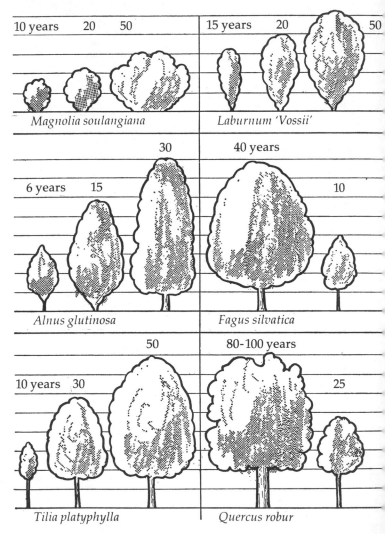

| 10 years | 20 | 50 | 15 years | 20 | 50 |

Magnolia soulangiana *Laburnum 'Vossii'*

| 30 | 40 years |
| 6 years | 15 | | 10 |

Alnus glutinosa *Fagus silvatica*

| 50 | 80-100 years |
| 10 years | 30 | | 25 |

Tilia platyphylla *Quercus robur*

Growth and development of selected plants (horizontal lines in 2 meter increments)

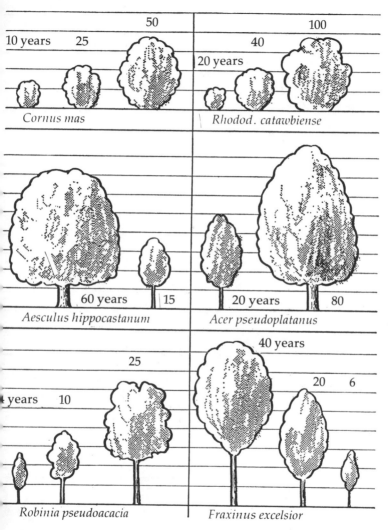

10 years	25	50	
Cornus mas

20 years	40	100
Rhodod. catawbiense

60 years	15	
Aesculus hippocastanum

20 years	80	
Acer pseudoplatanus

years	10	25
Robinia pseudoacacia

40 years	20	6
Fraxinus excelsior

Growth and development of selected plants (horizontal lines in 2 meter increments)

Age & Height

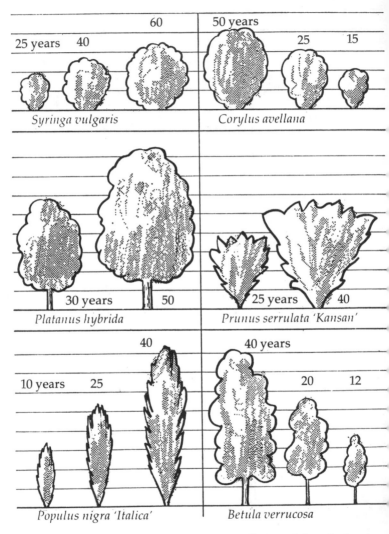

Growth and development of selected plants (horizontal lines in 2 meter increments)

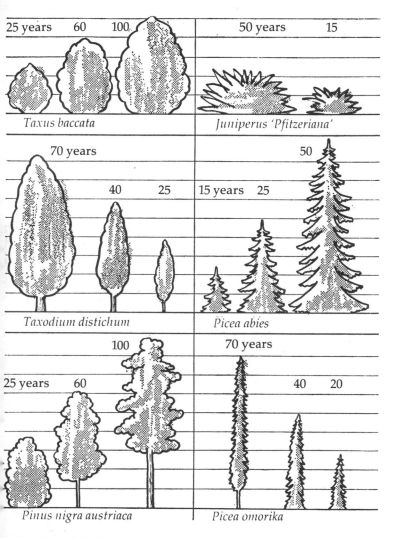

25 years   60   100

50 years   15

Taxus baccata

Juniperus 'Pfitzeriana'

70 years

50

40   25

15 years   25

Taxodium distichum

Picea abies

100

70 years

25 years   60

40   20

Pinus nigra austriaca

Picea omorika

Growth and development of selected plants (horizontal lines in 2 meter increments)

Specimen Plants

Ribes sanguineum			
'Atrorubens'	fl	zone 5	dark red flower
— — 'Edward VII'	fl		as above
Rosa, park or shrub roses	fl fr		see list p. 53
Skimmia japonica	of fl fr #	7	good foliage
Spiraea nipponica	fl	4	white flower
— *sargentiana*	fl	5	as above
— *veitchii*	fl	5	as above
Staphylea colchica	fl fr	6	white flower
Stranvaesia davidiana	of fl #	6	white flower, red fruit
Syringa amurense	fl	4	flower white, very late
— *chinensis*	fl	5	lilac flower
— — 'Saugeana'	fl		violet red
— *meyeri*	of fl	5	lilac, dwarf plant
— *reflexa*	fl	5	rose red
— *sweginzowii* 'Superba'	fl	5	pink-white
— *tigerstedtii*	fl	5	abundant, pink-white
— *vulgaris*	fl	3	see list p. 55
Viburnum burkwoodii	of fl F	5	white, fragrant
— *carlcephalum*	fl F	5	as above
— *carlesii*	fl F	4	as above
— *dilatatum*	of fl fr	5	red fruit, good foliage
— *juddii*	of fl F	5	pink-white
— *macrocephalum*	fl	6	round white flower
— *opulus* 'Xanthocarpum'	fl fr	3	yellow fruit
— *plicatum*	fl	4	white, flat flower
— *prunifolium*	of fl fr	3	clean foliage, flower and fruit
— *rhytidophyllum*	of fl fr #	5	white flowers, red and black fruit
— *sieboldii*	of fl fr	4	white, good red fall color
— *tinus*	of fl fr #	7	white flower, blue fruit
Weigela spp.	fl		pink, red, white
— *florida* 'Foliis Purpuriis'	of fl	5	good purple foliage

CONIFERS

Trees

Abies concolor	#	4	gray-green, fragrant
— *homolepis*	#	4	green
— *nordmanniana*	#	4	dark green
— *pinsapo*	#	6	green to blue green
— *procera* 'Glauca'	#	5	silver-gray
— *veitchii*	#	3	needle underside white
Araucaria araucana	of #	7	stout branches, exotic
Cedrus atlantica 'Glauca'	#	6	blue-green
Chamaecyparis lawsoniana	#	5	dark blue-green
— *nootkatensis* 'Pendula'	#	4	pendulous branches
Gingko biloba	of	4	fan shaped foliage
Larix spp.	of		yellow-orange fall color
Picea abies	#	5	dark green
— — 'Viminalis'	#		pendulous branch tips

— *breweriana*	#	zone 5	foliage hangs vertically
— *omorika*	fr #	4	narrow columnar
— *orientalis*	#	4	deep green
— *pungens*	#	2	blue-green
— — 'Glauca'			blue-white, silvery
Pinus cembra	#	4	strictly conical
— *leucodermis*	#	5	deep green
— *nigra austriaca*	#	4	long bright green needles
— *peuce*	#	4	broadly conical
— *ponderosa*	#	5	very long needles
— *silvestris*	#	2	reddish bark with age
— *strobus*	#	3	rapid grower, fine needles
— *wallichiana*	#	5	long soft needles
Psuedolarix amabilis	of	5	gold-yellow fall color
Psuedotsuga menziesii	#	5	fast growing
Sciadopitys verticillata	#	5	thick needles in whorls
Taxodium distichum		4	tolerates standing water
Taxus baccata	#	6	tolerates deep shade
Thuja occidentalis	#	2	good as hedge
— *plicata*	#	5	rapid, cone shape
Thujopsis dolabrata	#	6	needle undersides white
Tsuga canadensis	#	4	fast growing, shade tolerant
— *heterophylla*	#	6	fast growing
— *mertensiana*	#	5	blue-green foliage

Shrubs, 3—5m high

Chamaecyparis nootkatensis			
'Lutea'	#	4	yellow-green
— *obtusa* 'Crippsii'	#	3	good yellow
— *pisifera* 'Filifera'	#	3	fine textured, dense
— — 'Filifera Aurea'	#		as above, yellow
Cryptomeria japonica 'Elegans'	#	5	blue-green
Juniperus chinensis 'Hetzii'	#	4	upright, blue-green
— — 'Pfitzeriana'	#		broad, green
— — 'Pfitzeriana Aurea'	#		as above, yellow tips
— *communis*	#	2	broadly columnar
— — 'Oblongo-pendula'	#		irregular, pendulous
— — *hibernica*	#		narrowly columnar
— — 'Suecica'	#		as above
— *virginiana* 'Burkei'	#	2	broadly columnar, blue
— — 'Canaertii'	#		wide, upright, deep green
— — 'Schottii'	fr #		as above
— — 'Glauca'	#		broad upright, silver-blue
Pinus mugo	#	2	broad rounded
Taxus baccata			
'Adpressa Stricta'	#	6	strict upright
— — 'Aureovariegata'	#		yellow foliage
— — 'Dovastoniana'	#		broad horizontal branching
— — 'Fastigiata'	#		broadly columnar
Taxus cuspidata	#	4	broad pyramidal
— *media* 'Hicksii'	#	4	upright, good hedge

Specimen Plants

Shrubs 150—300cm

Chamaecyparis lawsoniana			
'Ellwoodii'	#	zone 5	fine texture, blue-green
— — 'Filiformis'	#		fine branches
— — 'Fletcheri'	#		fine texture, blue-gray
— — 'Lycopoides'	#		coarse, deep green
— — 'Minima Glauca'	#		broad oval, blue-green
— — 'Glauca'	#		broad, blue-green
— *obtusa*	#	3	broadly conical, deep green
— — 'Pygmaea'	#		rounded, brownish
— *pisifera* 'Filifera'	#	3	threadlike foliage, green
Cryptomeria japonica			
'Jindai-sugi'	#	5	dense conical
Juniperus chinensis			
'Blaauwi'	#	4	coarse, gray-green
— × *media* 'Plumosa'	#	4	coarse textured, green
— — 'Plumosa Aurea'	#		as above, but yellow
— *sabina*	#	4	upright or creeping
— *squamata* 'Meyeri'	#	4	coarse, silver-blue
virginiana 'Tripartita'	#	2	blue-green
Picea abies 'Compacta'	#	5	dense, wide conical
— — 'Nidiformis'	#		low nest form
— — 'Ohlendorffii'	#		broadly conical
— — 'Pygmaea'	#		dense upright
— *glauca* 'Conica'	#	2	dense little cone
— *omorika* 'Nana'	#	4	broadly conical
Picea orientalis			
'Gracilis'	#	4	broad oval
Pinus mugo pumilio	#	2	dense, cushion form
— *silvestris* 'Watereri'	#	2	broad oval, blue
Taxus baccata 'Adpressa'	#	6	bushy, green
— — 'Adpressa Aurea'	#		as above, yellowish
— *cuspidata* 'Nana'	#	4	wide, dark green
— *media* 'Thayerae'	#	4	wide, long needles
— — 'Runyun'	#		compact bush form
— — 'Wardii'	#		lower spreading type
Thuja occidentalis			
'Ellwangeriana Aurea'	#	2	bushy, yellow to copper
Tsuga canadensis 'Albospica'	#	4	branch tips white

4. Economical Plants

Here follows a small list of plants, easy to obtain and requiring little care.

Buddleia alternifolia, zone 5
    lilac fl cf
— davidii var. 5 fl cf
Calycanthus floridus, 4 F
    cinnamon red fl cf fr
Cercis canadensis, 4 of fl
Chaenomeles japonica, 4
    red fl cf fr
— speciosa, 4 red fl cf fr
Cornus florida, 4 white fl cf of
— kousa, 4 white fl cf
Cotinus coggygria, 5 fl fr
Cotoneaster spp. white fl fr
Crataegus phaenopyrum, 4 white fl fr
Cytisus scoparius, 5 S
    yellow to red fl
— praecox, 5 S bright yellow fl
Deutzia magnifica, 5 white fl cf
— scabra 'Plena', 5 white fl cf
Forsythia intermedia, 5 yellow fl cf
— suspensa, 5 yellow fl cf
Genista tinctoria, 2 yellow fl
Hibiscus syriacus, zone 5
    lilac, white, red fl
Hydrangea arborescens
'Grandiflora', 4 white fl cf
— paniculata 'Grandiflora'
    4 white fl cf
Hypericum patalum henry,
    6 yellow fl
Jasminum nudiflorum, 5 yellow fl cf
Kolkwitzia amabilis, 4 light pink fl cf
Lespedeza thunbergii, 4 purple fl cf
Lonicera fragrantissima, 5
    F white fl cf F fr
— tatarica, 3 pink-whte fl
    cf F fr
— maackii, 2 white fl of cf fr
Magnolia soulangiana, 5
    pink-white fl cf ss
— stellata, 5 white fl cf
Malus, see list p. 59
    white, pink, red fl fr cf
Philadelphus coronarius, 4
    F white fl cf

Potentilla fruticosa, 2
    yellow or white fl
Prunus cerasifera
    'Thundercloud', 3 light pink fl cf
— glandulosa 'Alboplena, 4
white fl cf
— serrulata 'Kanzan', 5
    pink fl cf
— subhirtella 'Hally
    Jolivette', 5 white fl cf
— — 'Pendula', pink-red fl cf wg
Prunus triloba,5 pink fi
Rhododendron, see list p. 52
    fl cf
Ribes alpinum, 2 fr
— odoratum,4 yellow fl F
Robinia hispida, 5 lilac-pink fl
Rosa, see list p. 60 fl
Salix caprea, 4 yellow fl cf
— sachalinense 'Sekka', 4 of cf
Spirea arguta, 4 white fl cf
— bumalda 'Anthony Waterer'
    carmine fl cf
— — 'Gold Flame', yellow of
    pink fl cf
— douglasii, 5 red fl cf
— japonica 'Alpina', 5 pink-red fl
— nipponica 'Snowmound', 4 white fl
— prunifolia, 4 white fl cf
— vanhouttei, 4 white fl cf
Syringa chinensis, 5 F lilac fl cf
— villosa, 2 lilac to white fl
— vulgaris, see list p. 69
    lilac, white, blue, red fl cf
Tamarix parviflora, 4 pink fl cf
— pentandra, 2 pink, fl cf
Viburnum burkwoodii, 5 F white fl of cf
— dentatum, 2 white fl fr
— opulus 'Sterile', 3 white fl cf
— plicatum 'Mariesii', 4 white fl
Weigela 'Bristol Ruby', 5 red fl cf
Weigela florida zone 5
    'Purpurea'. lilac-pink fl
    red of cf
Weigela 'Newport Red', 5 red fl cf

5. Rock Garden Plants
a. Outstanding Dwarf Plants

BROADLEAVES

Acantholimon glumaceum	zone 7	# pink-red fl cr su
Aethionema grandiflorum	7	# pink fl su
Andromeda polifolia	2	# m ss cr fl
Arctostaphylos uva-ursi	2	# S H cf of su-ss
Arctous alpina	2	cr of S H su-ss
Astragalus angustifolius	6	fl su d
Berberis buxifolia 'Nana'	5	# of su-ss
— empetrifolia	5	# of fl su-sh
— stenophylla 'Corallina'	5	# of fl su-sh
— — 'Gracilis Nana'		# of su-sh
— thunbergii atropurpurea 'Nana'	4	of
Betula nana	3	m cr of su-ss
Bruckenthalia spiculifolia	5	# S H cr fl
Calluna var. see list p. 40		# S H cr fl
Calophaca wolgarica	4	cr fl su
Caragana jubata	2	S fl su
— pygmaea	2	S fl su
Cassiope lycopodioides	8	# H m cr fl ss
— tetragona	7	# H m cr fl ss
Chaenomeles speciosa sargentii	4	fl fr su
— — 'Simonii'		fl fr su
Clematis alpina	4	H cr ss-sh fl
Cornus canadensis	2	ss-sh fl of fr
Cotoneaster adpressus	4	cr of
— apiculata 'Tom Thumb'	4	of
— dammeri	5	# H m of fl fr su-sh
— — 'Mooncreeper'		# H of fl su-sh
— — radicans		# H m of fl fr su-sh
— horizontalis	4	cr fl fr of
— — 'Perpusillus'		cr fl fr of
— — 'Saxatilis'		cr fl fr of
— microphyllus	5	# cr of fr fl su-sh
— — 'Cochleatus'		# cr of fl fr su-sh
— salicifolius repandens	6	# cr fl fr of su-sh
Cytisus ardoinii	7	cr fl su
— beanii	5	d cr fl su
— decumbens	5	d cr fl su
— kewensis	6	d cr fl su
Daboecia cantabrica	5	# H cr fl
Daphne alpina	4	# F H fl su
— cneorum	4	# F C fl cr su-ss
— laureola	6	# H fl ss-sh
— retusa	4	# H fl ss
Dryas octopetala	4	# cr su fr fl
— suendermannii	4	# cr su fr fl
Empetrum nigrum	2	# cr su-sh fr

Erica, all see list p. 40		# cr
Erinacea pungens	zone 6	d cr fl
Euonymus fortunei	5	# u H cr of
— — 'Carrierei'		# u H cr of
— — 'Minimus' (='Kewensis')		# u H cr of
— — 'Vegetus'		# u H cr of fr
Forsythia viridissima 'Bronxensis'	5	of fl
Gaultheria miquelinana	5	# H S cr of fr
— *procumbens*	3	# H s cr of fr
— *shallon*	5	# H S cr of fl fr
Genista hispanica	6	d S cr fl
— *lydia*	5	d S fl
— *radiata*	6	d S fl
— *sagittalis*	6	d S cr fl
— — *minor*		d S cr fl
— *tinctoria* 'Plena'	2	d S cr fl
Hebe cupressoides	8	# of
— *hectori*	8	# of
Hedera helix 'Conglomerata'	5	# cr of
— — 'Erecta'		# cr of
— — 'Ovata'		# cr of
— — 'Sagittifolia'		# cl of
Helianthemum, all		cr fl
Iberis saxatilis	6	# cr fl
— *sempervirens*	5	# cr fl
Lavandula officinalis	5	# F d fl of su
Ledum groenlandicum	2	# F m fl of
— *palustre*	2	# F m fl of
Leiophyllum buxifolium	5	# d cr fl of
Lithospermum spp.		H cr fl ss
Mahonia repens	5	# cr fl fr ss-sh
Microbiota decussata	2	# of
Moltkia petraea	6	d fl su
Muehlenbeckia nana	7	# cr of
Olearia haastii	8	# of
— *nummulariaefolia*	8	# of
Paxistima canbyi	5	# of fl fr m
Penstemon menziesii	5	fl su
— *scouleri*	5	fl su
Phyllodoce coerulea	2	# H m cr fl ss
— *empetriformis*	4	# H m cr fl of ss
Polygala chamaebuxus	4	# d fl su
Potentilla arbuscula	2	cr fl su
— *dahurica*	2	cr fl su
— *mandschurica*	2	cr fl su
— *tridentata*	2	# fl su-ss cr
Prunus prostrata	6	cr fl su
— *pumila depressa*	4	cr fl su
Rhamnus alpinus	4	of su
— *pumilus*	4	cr of su
Rhododendron, see list p. 42		
— *ferrugineum*	4	# H cr fl su

Rock Garden Plants

— *forrestii repens*	zone 4	# H m cr fl su-ss
— *hirsutum*	4	# A fl su
— *impeditum*	4	# H F fl ss
—, japanese Azaleas see list p.45		
— *keleticum*	4	# H cr fl su-ss
Rhododendron myrtilloides	4	# H fl ss
— *radicans*	4	# H m cr fl su-ss
— 'Ramapo'	4	# H fl su
— 'Purple Gem'	4	# H fl su
Salix arbuscula	3	m of cr su
— *cottetii*	3	m of cr su
— *lanata*	3	m of cr fl su
— *repens*	4	m of cr su
— *reticulata*	2	m-w of cr
— *retusa*	3	m of cr su
Santolina, all		# F fl of su
Satureja montana	4	F fl cr su
Spirea decumbens	4	fl cr su
— *x bumalda*	5	fl su
— *japonica alpina*	5	fl su
— *lancifolia*	4	fl cr su
Teucrium chamaedrys	5	fl of su
Viburnum opulus 'Nana'	3	of su-sh
— *plicatum tomentosum* 'Newport'	4	fl su

CONIFERS

Abies koreana 'Prostrata'	5	# su
Chamaecyparis pisifera 'Nana'	3	# ss of
— — 'Nana Aurea'		# ss of
Ephedra spp.		# cr su-ss of fr
Juniperus communis 'Compressa'	2	# su of
Juniperus communis		
'Hornbrookii'	2	# cr su of
— — 'Repanda'		# cr su of
— *horizontalis*	3	# cr su of
— — 'Douglasii'		# cr su of
— — 'Glauca'		# cr su of
— *procumbens*	5	# cr su of
— — 'Nana'		# cr su of
— *virginiana* 'Reptans'	2	# cr su of
Picea abies 'Gregoryana'	5	# su-ss of
— *Glauca* 'Echiniformis'	2	# su-ss of

b. Larger Plants for the Rock Garden

BROADLEAVES

Acer japonicum 'Aureum', zone 5 H of
— — 'Filicifolium' H of
— — 'Vitifolium' H of
— *palmatum*, 5 H of
— — 'Atropurpureum', H of
— — 'Dissectum', H of
Aesculus mutabilis induta 6 fl
Atraphaxis billardieri, 7 S d fl su
— *frutescens*, 7 S d fl su
Atriplex canescens, 7 S d fl of
Berberis buxifolia, 5 # H fl of ss fr
— *candidula*, 5 # H fl of ss
Berberis julianae, zone 5 # H fl of ss
— *verruculosa*, 5 # H fl of ss
— *wilsoniae*, 5 H fl fr su
Carpinus tschonoskii, 5 of su-ss
Caryopteris clandonensis, 7 fl su F S
— *incana*, 5 F S fl su
Cercis canadensis, 4 fl su
— *siliquastrum*, 6 fl su
Chaenomeles japonica, 4 fl fr su
— *speciosa*, 4 fl fr su
Comptonia asplenifolia, 2 F m H of ss
Cotoneaster dielsianus, 5 H fl fr of su-ss
Cotoneaster watereri 'Pendulus', zone 6,
    H wg of fl fr ss
— *salicifolius*, 6 # H fr of fl
— — *floccosus*, # H fr of fl
Crataegus orientalis, 5 d fl of fr
Cytisus praecox, 5 d S fl
— — 'Albus' d S fl
— *purpureus*, 5 d S fl
— *scoparius*, 5 d S fl
Daphne cneorum, 4 # C F fl su-ss
— *burkwoodii*, 5 H fl su
— — 'Somerset', H fl su
— *mezereum*, 4 H fl su-ss fr
— — 'Album', 4 H fl su-ss fr
Deutzia gracilis, 4 H fl cf su
Disanthus cercidifolius 6 H of ss
Euonymus japonicus, 8 u # of
— *alatus* 'Compacta', 3 of su
— *nanus*, 4 H u of fr
— — *turkestanicus*, 4 H u of fr
Fuchsia gracilis, 7 H u fl ss-sh
— — 'Riccartoniana' H u fl ss-sh
Halesia carolina, 4 fl su-ss
Hydrangea involucrata, 5 m H fl

— *anomala petiolaris*, 4 m H fl cl
— *quercifolia*, 5 H m fl of
— *aspera macrophylla*, 7 m H fl of
Hypericum calycinum, 6 # fl cr H S su-sh
— 'Hidcote', # H fl su
— *moserianum*, 7 H fl su fr
— *patulum*, 6 H fl su
— 'Rowallane', # H fl su
Ilex crenata, 6 # H u of
— — 'Convexa', H # of su-ss
Jasminum nudiflorum, 5 H fl cf su
Kalmia angustifolia, 2 # m H fl ss
Koelreuteria paniculata, 5 fl of fr
Ligustrum japonicum
    'Rotundifolium, 7 # of ss
— *vulgare* 'Lodense, 4 of su
Lonicera alpigena, 5 fl fr ss
— *involucrata*, 'Humilis'1, 5 fl fr su-ss
— *nitida*, 7 # H of su-sh
— — 'Graziosa', # H of su-sh
— — 'Elegant'
— *pileata*, 5 # H of su-sh cr
— *spinosa alberti*, 5 fl of cr
— *syringantha*, 4 fl of su-ss
Magnolia sieboldii, 5 H fl of ss
— *soulangiana*, 5 H fl of ss
Pernettya mucronata, 7 # H fr of ss
Perovskia atriplicifolia, 4 F fl su d S
Philadelphus 'Miniature Snowflake',
    4 F fl su
Pieris forrestii, zone 8 H # fl ss-sh
— *floribunda*, 4 # S fl su-ss
— *japonica*, 5 # H fl su-ss
— *taiwanensis*, 7 # H fl ss-sh
Potentilla fruticosa, 2 d fl su
Prunus cistena, 2 C fl of
— *conradinae*, 8 fl ss
— *fruticosa*, 4 C fl of
— *pumila*, 4 C fl su
— *tenella*, 2 C fl su
— — 'Alba', C fl su
— *triloba*, 5 fl su
Rhus aromatica, 3 F m of fl
— *glabra*, 2 fl of fr su
Ribes alpinum 'Pumilum' 2 m H of su-sh
Rosa, miniature types see list p. 60
    fl su
— *rugosa* 'Repens Alba', 2 cr fl su

Rock Garden Plants

Ruscus aculeatus, 7 # u d of
— *hypoglossum*, 7 # u d of
Salix aurita, 3 m fl su-ss
— *caprea*, 4 m fl su-ss
— *hastata wehrhahnii*, 5 m fl su
Sarcococca ruscifolia, 7 # H of cr ss-sh
Skimmia japonica, 7 # H of fr ss
— *reevesiana* 'Rubella', 7 # of fl ss
Sorbus chamaemespilus zone 5 fl fr su
— *gracilis*, 5 fl fr su
— *koehneana*, 5 fl fr su-ss
— *prattii*, 5 fl fr su
— *vilmorinii*, 5 fl fr su
Spirea albiflora, 4 fl su
— *arguta*, 4 fl su
— *bumalda*, 5 fl su

— — 'Anthony Waterer' fl su
— — 'Crispa' fl su
— — 'Gold Flame' fl su of
— *japonica* 'Macrophylla', 5 fl su
— *nipponica*, 4 fl su
— *thunbergii*, 4 fl su
Stephanandra incisa, 5 fl of su
Syringa 'Miss Kim', zone 3 fl su
— *velutina*, 3 F fl su
Ulmus pumila, 4 H of
Viburnum davidii, 7 # m of sh fr
— *farreri* 'Nanum', 5 m fl of su
— *opulus* 'Compactum', 3 m of su fr
Vinca minor, 4 # fl su-sh
Zenobia pulverulenta, 5 F fl of ss
— — *nuda*, F fl of ss

CONIFERS

	zone		
Abies balsamea 'Nana'	3	# of	green
— — *hudsonia*		# of	dark green
— *procera* 'Glauca'	5	# of	silvery-gray
Cedrus atlantica 'Glauca'	6	# of	blue-gray
— — 'Pendula'		# of wg	blue-gray
— *libani*	5	# of	green
— — 'Sargentii'		# of cr	blue-gray
Chamaecyparis lawsoniana	5	# of	blue-green
— — 'Minima Glauca'		# of	blue-green
— — 'Tharandtensis Caesia'		# of	blue-gray
— — 'Fletcheri'		# of	blue-gray
— *nootkatensis* 'Pendula'	4	# of wg	blue-green
— *obtusa* 'Filicoides'	3	# of	moss green
— — 'Lycopodioides'		# of	blue-gray
— — 'Nana'		# of	fresh green
— — 'Nana Kosteri'		# of cr	yellow-green
— *pisifera* 'Filifera Nana'	3	# of	green, threadlike
— — 'Filifera Nana Aurea'		# of	yellow, threadlike
— — 'Dwarf Blue'		# of	blue-green
— — 'Plumosa Compressa'		# of	blue-green
— *thyoides* 'Andelyensis'	3	# of	blue green
Cryptomeria japonica			
'Bandai Sugi'	5	# of	dark green
— — 'Jindai Sugi'		# of	dark green
— — 'Elegans'		# of	blue-green, coarse
Juniperus conferta	5	# of cr	gray-green
— *chinensis* 'Plumosa'	4	# of	green
— — 'Plumosa Aurea'		# of	yellow
— — 'Blaauw'		# of	blue-green
— *horizontalis* 'Wiltoni'	2	# of cr	blue
— *procumbens nana*	5	# of cr	gray-green
— *sabina*	4	# of	dark green

— — 'Tamariscifolia'		# of cr	fresh green
— — 'Broadmore'		# of cr	gray-green
— *squamata* 'Meyeri'	4	# of	silver-blue
— — *wilsonii*		**# of**	**blue-gray**
Picea abies, **dwarf types**	5	# of	green
— *glauca* 'Conica'	2	# of	light green
Pinus sylvestris 'Watereri'	2	# of	blue-green
— *cembra*	4	# of	dark green
— *peuce*	4	# of	dark green
— *strobus* 'Nana'	3	# of	blue-green
— — 'Fastigiata'		# of	blue-green
— — 'Pendula'		# of wg	blue-green
— *densiflora* Umbraculifera'	4	# of	dark green
— *mugo*	2	# of	green
— — *mughus*		# of	green
— — *pumilio*		# of	green
Taxus baccata 'Repandens'	6	# of	green
— *cuspidata* 'Nana'	4	# of	green
Thuja occidentalis 'Globosa'	2	# of	green
— — 'Recurva Nana'		# of	dark green
Thujopsis dolabrata 'Nana'	6	# of	deep green
Tsuga canadensis 'Pendula'	4	# of wg	bright green

6. Trees for City Street

a. Trees for Open Suburban Areas

Recommended spacing given in meters. For soil requirements see p. 84.

Acer campestre, **zone 5**	6— 8m	*Populus canadensis*	
— *platanoides,* 3	8—10m	'Regenerata, **zone 4**	8—10m
— *psuedoplatanus,* 5	8—10m	— — 'Robusta'	7— 8m
— *saccharum,* 3	8—10m	— — 'Serotina'	8—10m
Aesculus hippocastanum, 3	8—10m	— *trichocarpa,* 4	8—10m
Ailanthus altissima, 4	8—10m	*Prunus avium,* 3	8—10m
Alnus glutinosa, 3	8—10m	*Quercus petraea,* 4	8—10m
— *incana,* 2	8—10m	— *robur,* 5	8—10m
Betula pubescens, 2	6— 7m	— *rubra* (=borealis), 4	10—12m
Catalpa **spp.**	8—10m	*Robinia psuedoacacia,* 3	7— 8m
Fagus silvatica, 4	8—10m	*Salix alba,* 2	6— 8m
Fraxinus excelsior, 3	8—10m	*Sorbus aria,* 5	6— 8m
Juglans regia, 5	8—10m	— *aucuparia,* 2	6— 8m
Populus alba, 3	8—10m	— *domestica,* 5	6— 8m
— *berolinensis,* 4	6— 8m	— *torminalis,* 5	6— 8m
— *canescens,* 4	8—10m	*Tilia platyphylla,* 3	8—10m
		Ulmus carpinifolia, 4	8—10m
		— *glabra,* 4	8—10m

Street Trees

b. Trees for Urban Areas
TALL, BROAD CROWNED TREES

Acer rubrum 'Autumn Flame' zone 3	8—10m	good habit and fall foliage
— — 'October Glory'	8—10m	as above
— — 'Red Sunset'	8—10m	as above
— *platanoides* 'Crimson King	8—10m	dark foliage, slow grower
— — 'Schwedleri'	8—10m	as above
— — 'Cleveland'	8—10m	good oval habit
— — 'Emerald Queen'	8—10m	as above
— — 'Summershade'	8—10m	as above
Aesculus carnea, 3	8—10m	good flower
Celtis occidentalis, 2	8—10m	subject to witches broom
— *laevigata*, 5	8—10m	resistant to w. broom
Corylus colurna, 3	7— 8m	industry tolerant
Fagus silvatica 'Atropunicea, 4	8—10m	not near industry
Fraxinus americana 'Autumn Purple', 3	8—10m	strong, good fall color
— *excelsior* 'Hessei', 3	8—10m	simple leaf, seedless
— *pennsylvanica* 'Marshall's Seedless', 2	8—10m	good foliage and shape
Gleditsia triacanthos inermis 'Imperial', 4	7— 8m	smaller, good form
— — — 'Moraine'	8—10m	wide, open
— — — 'Shademaster'	8—10m	tall oval
— — — 'Skyline'	8—10m	pyramidal
Gingko biloba, zone 4	7— 8m	plant only males
Carya ovata, 4	8—10m	needs deep fertile soil
Juglans cinerea, 3	8—10m	as above
Koelreuteria paniculata, 5	6— 8m	summer flowers
Liquidambar styraciflua 'Moraine', 5	8—10m	needs deep fertile soil
Liriodendron tulipifera, 4	8—10m	as above
Ostrya virginiana, 4	8—10m	slow growing
Phellodendron amurense, 3	8—10m	very wide habit
Platanus acerifolia, 5	10—12m	very industry tolerant
Populus simonii, 2	8—10m	quick growing
Quercus coccinea, 4	8—10m	open habit
— *imbricaria*, 5	8—10m	open, good foliage
— *phellos*, 6	8—10m	fine texture, open
Sophora japonica 'Regent', 4	8—10m	summer flowers
Sorbus intermedia, 5	6— 8m	needs deep fertile soil
— *latifolia*, 4	8—10m	fast, regular grower
Tilia euchlora, 5	7— 8m	excellent tree
— *cordata*, 3	8—10m	finer texture
— *petiolaris*, 5	8—10m	slightly pendulous
— *tomentosa*, 4	8—10m	white underleaf
Ulmus glabra 'Sarniensis, 4	8—10m	dense, conical
— *procera*, 5	8—10m	large oval
Zelkova serrata 'Village Green', 5	8—10m	wide V shape

c. Trees with Tall Narrow Crowns

Acer platanoides
  'Columnare', zone 3
— *pseudoplatanus* 'Erectum' zone 5
— *rubrum* 'Columnare', 3
— *saccharum* 'Temple's Upright', 3
Aesculus hippocastanum
  'Pyramidalis', 3 fl
Betula pendula 'Fastigiata' 2
Carpinus betulus
  'Fastigiata', 4
Crataegus monogyna 'Stricta'
  4 fl fr
Fagus silvatica
  'Fastigiata', 4
Gingko biloba 'Fastigiata' 4
Liriodendron tulipifera
  'Fastigiatum', 4

Malus 'Van Eseltine', 4 fl fr
Platanus acerifolia
  'Fastigiata', 5

Populus nigra 'Italica', 4
Prunus sargentii
  'Columnare', 4 fl
Quercus robur 'Fastigiata', 5
— *petraea* 'Columnaris', 4
Robinia psuedoacacia
  'Pyramidalis', 3 fl
Tilia platyphylla 'Fastigiata' 3
Ulmus carpinifolia 'Koopmanii', 4
— — 'Dampieri'
— — 'Sarniensis'
— *glabra* 'Exoniensis', 4

d. Trees with Small Round to Oval Crowns

Acer platanoides 'Globosum',
  zone 3
Aesculus hippocastanum
  'Umbraculifera', 3 fl
Carpinus betulus 'Globosa', 4
Crataegus lavallei, 4 fl fr
Crataegus monogyna inermis, 4 fl fr
— *phaenopyrum*, 4 fl fr
— *viridis* 'Winter King', 4 fl fr

Malus floribunda, 4 fl fr
— 'Snowdrift', 4 fl fr
Malus tschonoski, 4 fl fr
Prunus sargenti, 4 fl fr
Pyrus calleryana 'Bradford', 5 fl fr
Quercus turneri 'Psuedoturneri,
  6 # of
Robinia psuedoacacia 'Inermis', 3 of
— — 'Umbraculifera' of

e. Trees for Evergreen Avenues

Abies concolor, zone 4	5— 7m	apart
Chamaecyparis lawsoniana (and var.), 5	4— 5m	"
— *pisifera* (and tall forms), 3	4— 5m	"
Magnolia grandiflora, 7	5— 7m	"
Picea abies, 5	3— 5m	"
— *glauca*, 2	3— 5m	"
— *omorika*, 2	2— 3m	"
— *pungens*, 2	3— 5m	"
Pinus nigra austriaca, 4	5— 7m	"
— *silvestris*, 2	5— 7m	"
— *strobus*, 3	8—10m	"
Psuedotsuga menziesii, 5	5— 7m	"
Quercus ilex, 7	8—10m	"
— *suber*, 8	8—10m	"
Thuja plicata, 5	8—10m	"
— *occidentalis*, 2	2— 3m	"
Tsuga canadensis, 4	6— 8m	"

7. Plants for Hedges

Most woody plants will serve as a hedge or border depending on the purpose of the enclosure. However for an evenly trimmed, dense hedge, the number of suitable species is more limited.

a. Plants Needed per 1 linear meter of Hedge

Should the desired hedge be extra dense, the recommended numbers should be doubled and planted in two rows and staggered.

per 1m

Transplanted hedging material such as *Ligustrum* etc., 100—125 cm high and well branched .... 3 plants

Transplanted single stem plants such as *Carpinus, Fagus* etc., 100—125 cm high and well branched .... 5 plants

Seedlings, 1 to 3 years old such as *Crataegus*, etc., strong and branched .... 6—8 plants

For low border hedges such as *Iberis Teucrium, Lavandula* etc. .... 5—10 plants

b. Plants for Regular, Trimmed Hedges

Acer campestre, zone 5, 100—250 cm high, 50—70 cm wide, dense
— *ginnala*, 2, 100—200 cm high, 50—70 cm wide, dense
Buxus sempervirens, 5 #, 100—200 cm high, 50—100 cm wide
Carpinus betulus, 4, 150—300 cm high, 50—100 cm wide, dense
Chamaecyparis pisifera 'Plumosa', 3 #, 100—200 cm high, 30—50 wide
Cornus mas, zone 4, 150—200 cm high, 70—100 cm wide, spring flower
Crataegus oxycantha, 4, 150—200 cm high, 30—70 cm wide, dense
Fagus silvatica, 4, 200—400 cm high, 60—100 cm wide, holds brown foliage in winter
Ligustrum ovalifolium, 5 #, 100—150 cm high, 30—50 cm wide
— *vulgare*, 4, 100—150 cm high, 30—50 cm wide
— — 'Atrovirens', 100—150 cm high, 30—50 cm wide, evergreen to February
Prunus laurocerasus, 6 #, 100—120 cm high, 50—70 cm wide
Picea abies, 5 #, 70—150 cm high, 50—100 cm wide, not industry tolerant
Pyracantha coccinea, 6 #, 100—150 cm high, 30—60 cm wide, red fruit
Ribes alpinum, 2, 70—120 cm high, 30—50 cm wide, shade tolerant
Spirea vanhouttei, 4, 100—150 cm high, 30—60 cm wide, white flower
Taxus baccata, 6 #, 100—200 cm high, 50—100 cm wide, dense
— *media* (and var.) 4 #, 50-150 cm high, 30—100 cm wide

c. Plants for Impenetrable, Thorn Hedges

Acanthopanax spp. fr
Berberis spp. fl of
Chaenomeles spp. fl fr
Crataegus spp. fl fr
Eleagnus spp. S fl fr
Gleditsia triacanthos, zone 4 of
Halimodendron halodendron, 2 of fl
Hemiptelea davidii, 6 of
Hippophae rhamnoides, 3 of fr
Ilex aquifolium, 5 # of fr ss-sh
— *pernyi*, 6 # of fr ss-sh
Maclura pomifera, 5 of fr
Malus sargentii, 5 fl fr

— *transitoria*, 5 fl fr
Pyrus communis, 4 fl fr of
Poncirus trifoliata, 6 fl fr of
Pyracantha coccinea, 6 # fl fr
—— 'Kasan', # fl fr
Rhamnus davurica, 2 of fr
Robinia psuedoacacia, 3 F fl of
Rosa spp. F fl fr su
Rubus fruticosus, zone 4 fl of fr e su-sh
— *cockburnianus*, 4 fl fr of su-sh
Ulex europaeus, 6 S fl su of
Ziziphus jujube, 7 fr e

d. Tall Border Plants, 3—10m high and over

DECIDUOUS

Acer campestre, zone 5 of
— *ginnala*, 2 of
— *monspessulanum*, 5 of
— *tataricum*, 4 of
Amelanchier x grandiflora
   zone 4 fl of fr ss
— *laevis*, 4 fl of fr ss
— *ovalis*, 4 fl of fr ss
Caragana arborescens, 2 S
   fl of
Carpinus betulus, 4 of
Cornus mas, 4 fl fr of
Corylus avellana, 3 fl fr e
   ss-sh
Cotinus coggygria, 5 of fl fr
Crataegus coccinea, 5 fl fr of
— *phaenopyrum*, 4 fl fr of

Crataegus crusgalli, zone 4
   fl fr of
— *monogyna*, 4 fl fr of
Eleagnus angustifolia, 2 fl of
Fagus silvatica, 4 of
Lagerstroemia indica, 7 fl
Maclura pomifera, 5 fr
Malus baccata, 2 fl fr
— *floribunda*, 4 fl fr
Populus berolinensis, 4 of
— *nigra* 'Italica', 4
— *canadensis* 'Robusta', 4 of
Prunus mahaleb, 6 fl fr of
— *spinosa*, 4 fl fr of
— *virginiana*, 2 fl fr of

BROADLEAF EVERGREENS

	zone	
Camellia japonica	5	# fl of
Ilex aquifolium	5	# H of fr su-sh
—— 'Pyramidalis'		# H of fr su-sh
Nerium oleander	7	# fl of
Prunus laurocerasus	6	# of
Rhododendron catawbiense	4	# H fl of
— *ponticum*	5	# H fl of
Stranvaesia davidiana	7	# fl fr su-sh

Hedges 2—4m high

CONIFERS

Chamaecyparis lawsoniana			
'Alumni	zone 5	# of	blue-green
— — 'Monumentalis'		# of	blue-green
— — 'Silver Queen'		# of	silver-gray
— — 'Triomf van Boskoop'		# of	blue-gray
— *pisifera* 'Plumosa'	3	# of	green
— — 'Squarrosa'		# of	blue-green
Larix decidua	2	of	bright green
— *kaempferi*	7	of	bluish green
Picea abies	5	# of	not industry tolerant
— *glauca*	2	# of	bluish green
— *omorika*	2	# of fr	Dark green
Pinus nigra	4	# of	bright green
— *strobus*	3	# of	green
— *sylvestris*	2	# of	blue-green
Pseudotsuga menziesii	5	# of	dark green
Taxus baccata	6	# of fr su-sh	dark green
— *cuspidata*	4	# of fr su-sh	dark green
Thuja occidentalis (and var.)	2	# of	dark green, in winter brown
— *plicata*	5	# of	dark green
Tsuga canadensis	4	# of su-sh	likes trimming
— *heterophylla*	6	# of su-sh	likes trimming

e. Hedges from 2—4m high

DECIDUOUS

Acanthopanax spp. of
Acer campestre, zone 5 of
Caragana arborescens, 2 S fl of
Calycanthus floridus, 4 of fl F
Carpinus betulus, zone 4 of su-sh
Chaenomeles speciosa, 4 fl fr
Cornus mas, 4 fl fr su-sh
— *sanguinea*, 4 fl fr su-sh
Corylus avellana, 3 of e su-sh
Cotoneaster bullatus, 5 fl fr of
— *dielsianus*, 5 fl fr of
— *divaricatus*, 5 fl fr of
— *multiflorus*, 5 fl fr of
— — *calocarpus* fl fr of
Crataegus oxycantha, 'Plena' zone 4 fl fr of
— — 'Paul's Scarlet' fl fr of
— *phaenopyrum*, 4 fl fr of
Deutzia scabra (and var.), 5 fl of

Eleagnus pungens, 7 of fl F
— *umbellatus*, 3 of fl F
Euonymus alatus, 3 of
— *europaeus*, 3 of fr su-sh
Fagus silvatica, 4 of
Forsythia intermedia, 5 fl of su-sh
— *suspensa*, 5 fl of wg su-sh
Hamamelis vernalis, 4 fl of
— *virginiana*, 4 fl of
Hibiscus syriacus, 5 fl
Kolkwitzia amabilis, 4 fl
Lonicera tatarica, 3 fl fr
— *xylosteum*, 4 fl fr su-sh
— *maackii*, 2 of fl fr
Ligustrum obtusifolium regelianum, 3 of fl
— *ovalifolium*, 5 # of fl
— *vulgare*, 4 of fl fr

Malus sargentii, 5 fl fr
Morus alba, 4 of fr
Philadelphus coronarius, 4 F fl of
— *grandiflorus*, 4 F fl of
— *inodorus*, 5 fl of
Physocarpus opulifolius, 2 fl of
Prunus besseyi, 3 fl fr
— *cistena*, 2 fl fr of
— *maritima*, 3 fl fr
Rhamnus catharticus, 4 of fr
— *frangula*, 2 of fr
Ribes sanguineum, 5 fl of su-sh
Rosa moyesii, 5 fl fr of
— *rubrifolia*, 2 fl fr of
— *rugosa*, 2 fl fr

Sambucus racemosa, 4 m H fr of ss-sh
Spirea vanhouttei, 4 fl of
Syringa chinensis, 5 F fl of su
— *villosa*, 2 fl of
— *vulgaris*, 3 F fl of su
Viburnum dentatum, 2 fl fr of
— *dilatatum*, 5 of fl fr
— *lantana*, 3 of fl fr
Viburnum opulus, zone 3 m fl fr of
— *prunifolium*, 3 fl fr of
— *setigerum*, 5 fl fr of
Viburnum trilobum, 2 fl fr of
Weigela florida, 5 fl
Zenobia pulverulenta, 5 of fl

BROADLEAF EVERGREENS

Arundinaria japonica, zone 6 # of
— *murielae*, 6 # of
— *nitida*, 6 # of
Choisya ternata, 7 # of fl F
Cotoneaster salicifolius, 6 # fl fr of
Ilex aquifolium, 5 # H of fr

Ligustrum ovalifolium, 5 # of fl
Prunus laurocerasus, 6 # of su-sh
Pittosporum tobira, 8 # of fl
Pyracantha coccinea, 6 # of fr
Rhododendron catawbiense, 4 # fl of
Stranvaesia davidiana, 6 # fl fr su-sh

CONIFERS

Chamaecyparis lawsoniana	zone 5	#	green to blue-green
— — 'Alumnii'		#	blue-green
— *pisifera* 'Plumosa'	3	#	dark green, fine texture
— — 'Squarrosa'		#	blue-gray
Juniperus chinensis	4	#	gray to green
Picea abies	5	#	not industry tolerant
Pinus mugo	2	#	dark green
Taxus baccata	6	#	dark green
— *media* 'Hicksii'	4	#	dark green
Thuja occidentalis (and var.)	2	#	dark green, brown in winter

Hedges 1—2m high

f. Hedges from 1—2m high

DECIDUOUS

Berberis mentorensis	zone 5	fl of	red fall foliage
— *thunbergii*	4	fl fr of	
—— 'Atropurpurea'		fl fr of	red foliage
Carpinus betulus 'Fastigiata'	4	of	
Chaenomeles spp.		F fl fr e of	
Cotoneaster		fl fr of	
— *dielsianus*	5	fl fr of	
— *divaricatus*	5	fl fr of	
— *franchetii*	6	fl fr of	
Forsythia 'Arnold's Dwarf'	5	of	
Kerria japonica 'Plena'	4	fl of	
Ligustrum obtusifolium,	4	of fl fr	
—— *regelianum*		fl fr of	
— *vulgare*	4	fl fr of	
—— 'Atrovirens'		of fr	
—— 'Lodense'		of	
Philadelphus lemoinii (and var.)	5	fl	
Prunus glandulosa	4	fl	
Ribes alpinum	2	m of fr su-sh	
— *sanguineum*	5	m fl su-sh	
Rosa rugosa	2	S fl fr of e	
Spirea arguta	4	fl of	
— *prunifolia*	4	fl of	
— *thunbergii*	4	fl of	
— *vanhouttei*	4	fl of	
— *nipponica*	4	fl of	
Stephanandra incisa	5	fl of	
Symphoricarpos chenaultii	4	fl fr of	
Syringa meyeri	5	fl	
Weigela florida 'Purpurea'	5	fl of	
—— 'Bristol Ruby'		fl	
Viburnum carlesii	4	fl F	
— *opulus* 'Compacta'	2	fl fr of	
— *trilobum* 'Compactum'	2	fl fr of	

BROADLEAF EVERGREENS

Abelia grandiflora	zone 5	# fl of
Berberis stenophylla	5	# H fl of
— *julianae*	5	# H of fl
— *sargentiana*	5	# H fl of
Buxus sempervirens	5	# of su-sh
Cotoneaster wardii	6	# H fl of fr
Ilex crenata	6	# H of fr
— *glabra* 'Compacta'	3	# of fr

Leucothoe fontanesiana	zone 4	# H of fl su-sh
Lonicera nitida 'Elegant'	7	# of fr su-sh
Osmanthus heterophyllus	6	# F fl of su-sh
Phillyrea vilmoriniana	6	# fl of su-sh
Pieris floribunda	4	# of fl
— japonica	5	# of fl
Prunus laurocerasus (and var.)	6	# of fl su-sh
— — 'Schipkaensis Macrophylla'		# of fl su-sh
— — 'Zabeliana'		# of fl su-sh
Pyracantha coccinea	6	# of fr fl
Rhododendron, see list p. 46		
Skimmia japonica	7	# of fl fr
Stranvaesia davidiana	6	# H fl of fr su-sh
Viburnum burkwoodii	5	# F H fl of
— rhytidophyllum	5	# H of fl fr su-sh

CONIFERS

Chamaecyparis lawsoniana 'Ellwoodii'	zone 5	#	blue-green
— — 'Fletcheri'		#	blue-gray
— obtusa 'Crippsii'	3	#	yellow-green
— — 'Nana Gracilis'		#	deep green
— — 'Tetragona Aurea'		#	gold-yellow
— thyoides 'Andelyensis'	3	#	blue-green
— — 'Ericoides'		#	gray-green
Juniperus communis hibernica	2	#	blue-green column
— — 'Suecica'		#	as above
— squamata 'Meyeri'	4	#	silver-blue
— virginiana 'Burkei'	2	#	blue-gray broad column
Picea glauca 'Conica'	2	#	light green, conical
Taxus baccata	6	#	dark green
— — 'Fastigiata'		#	as above
— cuspidata 'Densa'	4	#	low wide
— media 'Everlow'	4	#	low wide
Thuja orientalis	6	#	fresh green

g. Hedges from 40—100cm high

(see also the dwarf plant list pp 15 & 106.)

DECIDUOUS

Aronia melanocarpa	zone 4	of fl fr
		ss-sh
Artemesia abrotanum	5	F d S of
Chaenomeles japonica		
(and var.)		fl fr of e
Cotoneaster adpressa praecox		
	4	d fl cf fr of
— *apiculata*	4	of fr
Cytisus austriacus	5	d fl of
Deutzia gracilis	4	fl of
— *lemoinei*	4	fl of
— *rosea* (and var.)	5	fl of
Hypericum 'Hidcote'	6	# fl
— *moserianum*	7	fl of su-sh
— *patulum* (and var.)	6	fl of su-sh
Ligustrum vulgare 'Lodense'	4	of
Lonicera alpigena 'Nana'	5	of fr
— 'Clavey's Dwarf'	4	of fl
Myrica pensylvanica	2	F m H fr of
Philadelphus lemoinei	5	F fl of
Potentilla fruticosa (and var.)	2	fl (flowers all summer)
Prunus tenella	2	d A fl of
Ribes alpinum 'Pumilum'	2	m H of fr
Rosa nitida	3	fl of fr
— *chinensis* 'Minima'	5	fl of
— Tea Hybrids		F fl cf of fr
— Polyantha types		F fl cf of fr
— *pimpinellifolia* (and var.)	7	F fl cf of fr
Spirea albiflora	4	fl of
— *bumalda* 'Anthony Waterer'	5	fl of
— 'Froebelii'	5	fl of
— *nipponica* 'Snowmound'	4	fl of
Symphoricarpos 'White Hedge'	3	fr of fl
— *orbiculatus*	2	fr of fl
— 'Mother of Pearl'	3	fr of fl
Ulex europaeus	6	d S fl of

BROADLEAF EVERGREENS

Berberis buxifolia 'Nana'	zone 5	# of
— *hookeri* 'Compacta'	6	# of fl fr
— *verruculosa*	5	# fl of fr
Buxus sempervirens		
'Suffruticosa'	5	# su-sh of
— *microphylla* 'Compacta'	5	# su-sh of

Calluna vulgaris (and var.)	4	# S d fl of
Euonymus fortunei	5	# m H of cl cr su-sh
— — 'Gracilis'		# m H of cl cr su-sh
— — 'Sarcoxie'		# m H of cl cr su-sh
— *japonicus* 'Pulchellus'	8	# of ss
Gaultheria shallon	5	# S H of fr fl su-sh
Ilex crenata 'Convexa'	6	# H of su-sh
— — 'Helleri'		# H of su-sh
Lavandula officinalis	5	# F d of fl su
Lonicera nitida	7	# of su-sh
— *pileata*	5	# of su-sh
Mahonia aquifolium	5	# fl fr of su-sh
— — 'Compacta'		# fl fr of su-sh
— *repens*	5	# fl fr of su-sh
Pernettya mucronata	7	# fr of ss
Rhododendron (Dwarf spp.) see list p. 46		

CONIFERS

Chamaecyparis lawsoniana 'Ellwoodii'	zone 5	# (trimmed!)	gray-blue
— *pisifera* 'Squarrosa'	3	# (trimmed!)	gray-blue
Juniperus virginiana 'Globosa'	2	#	green
Picea abies 'Nidiformis'	5	#	dark green
Pinus mugo pumilio	2	#	dark green
Thuja occidentalis 'Globosa'	2	#	dark green
— — 'Recurva Nana'		#	dark green

For hedges less than 40cm, see lists for:
    Rock Garden plants, pp. 106, 109
    Dwarf Conifers, p. 15
    Rhododendron, p. 46

8. Plants for Windbreaks

Windbreaks are all to often planted as dense, impenetrable windblocks. With a dense planting the wind is deflected up and over giving short range protection but generating a whirlwind effect which actually increases wind velocity, erosion and evaporation after a short distance (60m). A looser planting allows some wind to pass through, under and over thereby reducing the total wind velocity and diminishing soil erosion and crop evaporation for 10 to 20 times the height of the windbreak. At best a mixture of deciduous trees, shrubs and evergreens are planted in multiple rows or masses. The spacing of the trees should be roughly the diameter of the mature plants.

TREES

Acer platanoides, zone 3
— *psuedoplatanus*, 5
Alnus glutinosa, 3
— *incana*, 2
Betula pendula, 2
Celtis **spp**.
Eleagnus angustifolia, 2
Fagus silvatica, 4
Fraxinus americana, 3
— *excelsior*, 3
— *pennsylvanica*, 3
Larix decidua, 2
Maclura pomifera, 5
Picea abies, 5 #
— *glauca*, 2 #
— *pungens*, 2 #
Pinus nigra, 4 #
— *strobus*, 3 #
— *sylvestris*, 2 #
Populus alba, 3
— *berolinensis*, 4
— *nigra* 'Italica', 4
— *tremula*, 2
Quercus palustris, 4
Quercus robur, 5
— *rubra*, 3
Robinia psuedoacacia, 3 fl
Sorbus alnifolia, 5 fl fr
— *aucuparia*, 2 fl fr
Thuja occidentalis, 2 #
Tilia cordata, 3
— *platyphylla*, 3
Ulmus **spp**.

TALL SHRUBS

Acer campestre, zone 5
— *ginnala*, 2
— *tataricum*, 4
Amelanchier **spp**. fl fr
Caragana arborescens, 2 fl
Cornus mas, 4 fl
Corylus avellana, 3
Crataegus punctata, 4 fl fr
— *phaenopyrum*, 4 fl fr
— *oxycantha*, 4 fl
Eleagnus umbellata, 3 fl F
Kolkwitzia amabilis, 4 fl
Lagersroemia indica, 7 fl
Ligustrum vulgare, 4
Lonicera maackii, 2 fl fr
— *tatarica*, 3 fl fr
Malus **spp**. fl fr
Philadelphus coronarius, 4 fl
Pinus mugo, 2 #
Prunus cerasifera, 3
— *laurocerasus*, 6 #
— *spinosa*, 4 fl
Rhamnus frangula, 2 fr
Rosa canina, 3 fl 3
— *rugosa*, 2 fl e
— *rubiginosa*, 5 F fl e
Rubus fruticosus, 4 fl e
Salix **spp**.
Sambucus nigra, 5 fl e
— *racemosa*, 4 fr
Syringa villosa, 2 fl
— *vulgaris*, 3 fl F
Viburnum dentatum, 2 fl fr
— *lantana*, 3 of fl fr
— *rhytidophylloides*, 5 of fl fr
— *rufidulum*, 5 fl fr of

9. Groundcover Plants

This list includes some vines which are suitable as groundcovers if not allowed to climb.

DECIDUOUS

Akebia quinata	zone 4	4 cl semi-evergreen
Artemisia stelleriana	2	of silver-white
Chaenomeles japonica alpina	4	fl fr
Ceanothus americanus	4	fl su
Cornus canadensis	4	fl of fr su-sh
Cotoneaster adpressus	4	fl cr
— apiculata	4	fr cr
— horizontalis (and var.)	4	fr cr
Cytisus decumbens	5	d fl of su
Cytisus kewensis	6	d fl of su
⊢ procumbens	5	d fl of cr su
— purpureus	5	d fl of cr su
Diervilla lonicera	4	u H fl cr ss-sh
— sessilifolia	4	u H fl cr su-sh
Genista pilosa	5	fl su
— sagittalis	6	S d fl cr of su
Forsythia 'Arnold's Dwarf'	5	u of cr ss (blooms seldom)
Hydrangea petiolaris	4	H cl fl of
Lycium halimifolium	4	fl of fr cr cl
Menispermum canadense	4	cl of fr
Parthenocissus quinquefolia	3	cl of su-sh
— tricuspidata 'Lowii'	4	cl of su-sh
Potentilla arbuscula	2	fl
— fruticosa mandschurica	2	S H fl cr of su
Rhus aromatica	3	F m S H of su-ss
Rosa rugosa 'Repens Alba'	2	fl of su
— virginiana	3	m fl of fr su
— 'Max Graf'	3	fl su
— 'The Fairy'	5	fl su
—, all low Polyantha types		fl of fr su
—, all *wichuriana* types		fl of fr su
—, all dwarf roses		fl of su
Robinia hispida	5	fl of su cr
Rubus illecebrosus	5	m H S fl fr of cr ss-sh
— laciniatus	5	S d fl fr e of
Salix repens	4	4 S of cr
— tristis	2	S of wg
Stephanandra incisa 'Crispa'	5	of su-ss
Symphoricarpos orbiculatus	2	fr of cr
— chenaultii 'Hancock'	4	fr of cr
Viburnum opulus 'Nanum'	3	of ss-sh
Xanthorhiza simplicissima	4	of fl cr ss-sh

Groundcovers

BROADLEAF EVERGREENS

Andromeda polifolia	zone 2	# m cr fl of
Arctostaphylos uva ursi	2	# S cr fl of
Bruckenthalia spiculifolia	5	# S cr fl
Calluna vulgaris see list p. 40	4	# S d fl
Cotoneaster congestus	6	# cr of fl fr su
— *dammeri*	5	# cr of fl fr su-sh
— — *radicans*		# cr of fl fr su-sh
— *salicifolius*	6	# cr of fl fr su-sh
Daboecia cantabrica	5	# m H cr fl of
Dryas octopetala	4	# d cr fl of fr
Empetrum nigrum	2	# m H cr of su-sh
Erica spp. see list p. 50		# fl cr of su-ss
Euonymus fortunei	5	# H cr of su-sh
— — 'Gracilis'		# H cr of su-sh
— — 'Coloradus'		# H cr of su-sh
— — 'Minimus'		# H cr of su-sh
— — 'Vegetus'		# H cr cl of fr su-sh
Euonymus fortunei 'Silver Queen'	5	# H cr cl of su-sh
— — 'Carrierei'		# H cr cl of fr su-sh
Gaultheria procumbens	3	# H cr of fr ss-sh
— *shallon*	5	# H cr of fl fr ss-sh
Helianthemum spp.		# d cr su fl
Hedera colchica	5	# H cr cl of su-sh
— *helix* (and var.)	5	# H cr cl of su-sh
Hypericum calycinum	6	# d H S cr fl su-sh
Iberis sempervirens	5	# cr fl of su
Leiophyllum buxifolium	5	# S cr fl of su
Leucothoe fontanesiana	4	# H fl of ss-sh
Loiseleuria procumbens	2	# S cr fl of su
Lonicera henryi	4	# H cl fl of ss-sh
— *japonica halliana*	4	# H cl fl of ss-sh
Mahonia aquifolium	5	# fl fr of su-sh
— *repens*	5	# cr fl fr su-sh
Mitchella repens	3	# of fl fr
Muehlenbeckia nana	7	# H cr of ss
Pachistima canbyi	5	#
Pachysandra terminalis	5	# H of fl
Sasa veitchii	6	# d H S cr of ss
Teucrium chamaedrys	5	# fl of
Vaccinium angustifolium	2	# H S m cr fl of fr e
Vinca minor (and var.)	4	# cr fl of ss-sh
— *major*	7	# cr fl of ss-sh

CONIFERS

Juniperus communis			
'Depressa'	zone 2	#	green
— — 'Hornbrookii'		# cr	fresh blue-green

Juniperus communis			
'Repanda'	zone 2	# cr	green
— *chinensis sargentii*	4	# cr	dark green
— *conferta* 'Blue Pacific'	5	# cr	blue-green
— *horizontalis*	3	# cr	blue-green
— — 'Douglasii'		# cr	silver-gray
— — 'Bar harbor'		# cr	blue-green
— — *plumosa*		# cr	green, purple in winter
— — *wiltoni*		# cr	bluish
— *procumbens*	5	# cr	dark green
— — 'Nana'		# cr	silver-green
— *sabina* 'Broadmore'	4	# cr	light green
— — 'Tamariscifolia'		# cr	fresh blue-green
— *virginiana* 'Reptans'	2	# cr	blue-gray
Taxus baccata 'Repandens'	6	# cr	dark green
— — 'Repandens Aurea'		# cr	yellowish
— *media* 'Wardii'	4	#	dark green

10. Tolerance to Air Pollution

BROADLEAF EVERGREENS

Berberis buxifolia, zone 5	good to very good	# of fr
— — 'Nana'	good to very good	# of
— *gagnepainii*, 5	good to very good	# of fl
— julianae, 5	good to very good	# of fl
— *stenophylla*, 5	good to very good	# of fl
Buxus sempervirens, 5	good to very good	# of
Calluna vulgaris see list p. 40	good to very good	#
Cotoneaster conspicuus, zone 6	good to very good	# fl fr cr
— *dammeri*, 5	good to very good	# fl fr of
— *henryanus*, 7	good to very good	# u fl fr
— *microphyllus*, 5	good to poor	# fl fr of
— *salicifolius floccosus*, 6	good to very good	# fl fr of
— *wardii*, 6	good to very good	# fl fr of
— *watereri*, 6	good to very good	# u fl fr of
Elaeagnus ebbingei, 6	good to very good	# u of
Erica carnea (and var.), 5	good; see list p. 40	
— *vagans* (and var.), 5	good; see list p. 40	
Euonymus spp.	good to very good	# H of cr
Gaultheria procumbens, 3	good to very good	# H of fr fl cr
— *shallon*, 5	good to very good	# H of fr fl cr
Hedera helix (and var.), 5	good to very good	# H cl cr of su-sh
Hypericum calycinum, 6	good to very good	# H fl cr su-sh
Ilex aquifolium, 5	good to very good	# H of fr su-sh
— *crenata*, 6	good to very good	# H of fr su-sh
— *glabra*, 3	good	# H m of fr su-sh
— *pernyi*, 6	good	# H of fr ss-sh

Industry Tolerant

Kalmia angustifolia, 2	good	# H fl of ss
— *latifolia*, 4	good to poor	# H m fl of ss
Leucothoe fontanesiana, 4	good to verygood	# H fl of ss-sh
Lonicera nitida, 7	good to very good	# H of ss-sh
— *pileata*, 5	good to very good	# H of su-sh
Magnolia grandiflora, 7	good to very good	# H of fl
Mahonia aquifolium, 5	good to very good	# H fl fr of
— *bealei*, 6	good to very good	# H fl fr of
— *japonica*, 6	good to very good	# H fl fr of
— *repens*, 5	good to very good	# H cr fl fr of
Osmanthus heterophyllus, 6	good to very good	# of fl fr su-ss
Osmarea burkwoodii, 6	good	# of fl ss
Pachysandra terminalis, 5	good	# H of fl ss-sh
Pernettya mucronata, 7	good to poor	# fr of su-ss
Phillyrea vilmoriana, 6	good	# H of fl ss
Pieris floribunda, 4	good to very good	# S fl of
— *japonica*, 5	good to very good	# H fl of
Prunus laurocerasus, 6	good to very good	# u of ss fl
— — 'Schipkaensis		
'Macrophylla'	good to very good	# u of ss fl
— — 'Otto Luyken'	good	# u H of
— — 'Zabeliana'	good to very good	# us H of
Pyracantha coccinea, 6	good to very good	# fl fr of
Quercus turneri		
'Psuedoturneri', 7	good	# of ss
Rhododendron fortunei, 6	good	# F H fl of ss-sh
— *laetevirens*, 4	good	# H of fl su-ss
— *williamsianum* (and var.), 6	good to very good	# H fl of ss-sh
for other Rhododendron hybrids see list p. 42		# fl of H
Sarcococca ruscifolia, 7	good	# H of ss-sh cr
Skimmia japonica, 7	good	# fr of ss
Stranvaesia davidiana, 6	good	# fl fr of su-sh
Viburnum davidii, 7	good to poor	# fl of fr
— *rhytidophyllum*, 5	good to very good	# fl of fr
Vinca minor, 4	good to very good	# fl of cr ss-sh
Zenobia pulverulenta, 5	good to very good	# F H fl cr

DECIDUOUS

A list of species in this category is unneccesary. Deciduous plants are generally much more tolerant of air pollution than evergreens. Any of them may be used provided they meet the other requirements of the site such as hardiness, soil type, etc. In general, one should avoid choosing those plants with thin, large or pubescent foliage. These qualities are more conducive to damage by smoke and soot, whereas a smaller, glossy leaf is easily cleansed by rain. Young foliage on warm and windy spring days is particularly susceptible to smoke and pollutant damage. Under such conditions one may notice browning of leaf margins, curling or spotting of leaves and/or total defoliation within 1

for other Rhododendron hybrids see list p. 42

to 2 days. In most cases these plants will refoliate, although most of the growing season will be lost. Also common is premature fall coloration and leaf drop, sometimes as early as late August/early September. In heavy industrial areas, only the most tolerant species should be used and then one should choose healthy, well developed specimens.

CONIFERS

Abies concolor, zone 4	#	best of the Firs
— *grandis*, 6	#	good in marginal conditions
— *koreana*, 5	#	as above
— *procera* 'Glauca'	#	as above
Araucaria araucana, 7	#	good in protected areas
Cedrus atlantica 'Gauca', 6	#	good to very good
Chamaecyparis, all	#	good to tolerance
Cryptomeria spp.	#	marginal use only
Ephedra	#	good
Ginkgo biloba, 4		good
Juniperus spp.	#	good to very good
— *chinensis* 'Pfitzeriana'	#	extremely good
Larix kaempferi, 7		good to very good
Metasequoia glyptostroboides, 5		good
Picea abies (and taller forms)	#	definitely **not** tolerant to gas or smoke
— *breweriana*, 5	#	good tolerance
— *jezoensis*, 4	#	not tolerant
— *omorika*, 4	#	best of the Spruce
— *orientalis*, 4	#	good in marginal areas
— *pungens*, (and var.), 2	#	most good to very good
Pinus cembra, 4	#	good to poor
— *densiflora*, 4	#	good
— *wallichiana*, 5	#	good
— *mugo* (and var), 2	#	good to very good
— *nigra austriaca*, 4	#	best of the Pines
Pinus parviflora, 5	#	good
— *silvestris*, 2	#	generally good
Pseudotsuga menziesii, 5	#	generally bad
Sciadopitys verticillata, 5	#	good to poor
Sequoiadendron gigantea, 6	#	good in marginal areas
Taxus baccata, 6	#	very good tolerance
— *cuspidata*, 4	#	very good
Thuja, all	#	good
Thujopsis dolabrata, 6	#	generally good
Tsuga canadensis, (and var.) 4	#	good in marginal cases
— *caroliniana*, 4	#	good
Taxodium distichum, 4		good

11. Dependable Species for Reclaiming Strip Mined Areas, Land Fills and Wasteland

Before planning from this list, soil pH must be determined, then the first planting should include pioneer species designated by *.

	Strip Mine reclamation	Land Fills, & Dump Sites	Sandy Wasteland	Sterile, Fine Sand	Gravelly Wasteland	
DECIDUOUS						
* Acer campestre, zone 5	—	×	×	—	—	not too dry
— platanoides, 3	—	—	×	×	×	not too dry
Ailanthus altissima, 4	—	×	×	—	—	takes dry soil
* Alnus glutinosa, zone 3	×	—	×	×	×	dislikes stagnant water
* — incana, 2	×	×	×	×	×	as above
Betula pendula, 2	×	×	×	×	×	full sun
Caragana arborescens, 2	—	×	—	×	—	withstands wind
Carpinus betulus, 4	—	×	×	—	—	sun or shade
Corylus avellana, 3	—	×	×	—	—	not too sandy
Crataegus spp.	—	×	—	×	—	clay, dry
Cytisus scoparius, 5	×	×	×	—	—	acid soil, full sun
Elaeagnus angustifolia, 3	—	×	×	—	—	dry soil
Fagus silvatica, 4	—	×	×	—	—	transplant in spring
Malus spp.	—	—	×	—	—	wind tolerant
* Populus alba, 2	—	—	×	—	×	wind and water tolerant
* — canescens, 4	—	×	×	×	×	as above
— canadensis, 4	—	—	×	—	—	not stagnant water
Prunus avium, 3	—	×	—	×	×	alkaline soil
— mahaleb, 6	—	×	—	—	—	alkaline, clay
* — serotina, 3	—	×	—	×	—	easily grown
— spinosa, 4	—	×	—	—	—	alklaine soil
Pyrus communis, 4	—	—	×	—	—	wind tolerant
Quercus cerris, zone 6	—	—	×	—	—	hot, dry areas
— petraea, 4	—	—	×	—	—	not too dry
— robur, 5	—	—	—	×	×	not too dry
— rubra, 4	—	—	×	×	—	strong grower
Rhus typhina, 5	—	×	—	—	—	fast grower
* Robinia pseudoacacia, 3	×	×	—	×	—	not for wet soil

128

	Strip Mine reclamation	Land Fills, & Dump Sites	Sandy Wasteland	Sterile, Fine Sand	Gravelly Wasteland	
Rosa canina, 3	—	×	×	—	—	not too dry
— rubiginosa, 5	—	×	—	—	—	strong grower
— multiflora, 5	—	×	—	—	—	clay soil
— rugosa, 2	—	×	—	—	—	not too dry
Rubus fruticosus, 4	—	—	×	—	—	wet or dry
Salix alba, 2	—	×	—	—	—	full sun
* —caprea, 4	×	×	×	—	×	very fast
* — daphnoides, 4	—	×	—	—	—	fast grower
— repens, 4	—	—	×	×	×	creeping shrub
Sambucus nigra, 5	—	×	×	—	—	clay soil
— racemosa, 4	—	×	—	—	—	dry or shady
Sorbus aucuparia, 2	—	—	×	×	—	good drainage
Spirea salicifolia, 5	×	—	—	—	—	not too dry
Tilia cordata, 3	—	—	×	—	—	not too wet
Symphoricarpos spp.	—	×	—	—	—	strong grower
Ulmus spp.	—	—	—	×	×	strong grower

CONIFERS

Picea abies, 5	—	—	×	—	—	clay soil
Pinus sylvestris, 2	—	×	×	×	×	takes wind
Larix kaempferi, 7	—	—	×	—	—	fast grower

12. Major Bee Attracting Plants

The number given represent months in bloom; thereby providing easy coordination of ornamental with fruit species to achieve maximum honey production and cross pollination. The most important plants are marked with an *.

Acer saccharinum, zone 3	2	3		
Alnus glutinosa, 3	2	3	4	
* Corylus avellana, 3	2	3		
Ulmus carpinifolia, 4	2	3		
Acer negundo, 2		3	4	
Alnus incana, 2		3	4	
Chaenomeles spp.		3	4	
* Cornus mas, 4		3	4	
* Erica carnea, 4	3	4	5
Daphne mezereum, 4	3	4	5
Populus alba, 2	3	4	
— canadensis, 4	3	4	
— nigra, 4	3	4	
— tremula, 2	3	4	5
Prunus padus, 3	3	4	
Ribes sanguineum, 5	3	4	5
* Salix caprea, 4	3	4	

Bee Attracting

Plant	Months
— *purpurea*, zone 3	3 4
Acer campestre, 5	4 5
— *platanoides*, 3	4 5
— *psuedoplatanus*, 5	4 5
Amelanchier, all	4 5
Berberis thunbergii, 4	4 5 6
* *Cercis canadensis*, 4	4
Cornus sanguinea, 4	4 5 6
Crataegus spp.	4 5
Forsythia spp.	4 5
Mahonia aquifolium, 5	4 5
Malus, fruit and simple flowering types	4 5
Paulownia tomentosa, 5	4 5
Prunus, all simple flowering types	4 5
— *avium*, 3 (sweet cherries)	4 5
— *cerasus*, 3 (sour cherries)	4 5
— *domestica*, 5 (plums)	4 5
* *Prunus mahaleb*, 6	4 5
* — *spinosa*, 4	4 5
* *Pyrus*, 4 (pears)	4 5
* *Ribes*, (gooseberry)	4 5
Sorbus aucuparia, 2	4 5
Aesculus carnea, 3	5
— *hippocastanum*, 3	5 6
Caragana spp.	5 6
Colutea spp.	5 6 7
Cotoneaster, all	5 6
Crataegus lavallei, 4	5 6
— *monogyna*, 4	5 6
Cytisus, most	5 6
Euonymus europaeus, 3	5 6
Exochorda spp.	5
Fraxinus ornus, 5	5 6
Iberis sempervirens, 5	5
Juglans regia, 5	5
Laburnum spp.	5 6
Lonicera, all	5 6
Lycium halimifolium, 5	6 7 8
Prunus serotina, 3	5—9
Rhamnus catharticus, 4	5 6
* *Rhamnus frangula*, 2	5 6 7
* *Robinia pseudoacacia*, 3	5 6,8 9
* *Rosa rugosa*, 2	5 6 7
Sorbus, most	5 6
Staphylea colchica, 6	5
* *Syringa*, spp.	5
Tamarix spp.	5 6 7
Viburnum spp.	5 6 7 8
Weigela spp.	5 6
Wisteria spp.	5 6
Ailanthus altissima, 4	6 7
Amorpha spp.	6 7 8
Castanea sativa, 5	6 7
Catalpa bignonioides, 4	6 7
Cladrastis lutea, 3	6
* *Eleagnus* spp.	6
Genista tinctora, 2	6 7 8
Gleditsia tricanthos, 4	6
Ligustrum vulgare, 4	6 7
* *Parthenocissus* spp.	6 7
Philadelphus spp.	6 7
Physocarpus pp.	6 7
Potentilla fruticosa, 2	6—10
Ptelea trifoliata, 4	6
Rhus typhina, 5	6 7
* *Rosa rubiginosa*, 5	6 7
— all garden roses	6—10
* *Rubus fruticosus*, 4	6 7
Sorbaria, all	6 7
Spirea, most	6 7 8
Stephanandra spp.	6
Stranvaesia davidiana, 6	6
Symphoricarpos spp.	6 7 8
* *Tilia cordata*, 3	6 7
* — *platyphylla*, 3	6 7
Vaccinium myrtillus, 2	6 7
— *vitis idaea*, 2	6
Aesculus parviflora, 4	7 8
* *Calluna vulgaris*, 4	7 8 9
Clematis vitalba, 4	7 8 9
Clethra alnifolia, 3	7 8
Holodiscus discolor, 5	7
Hypericum calycinum, 6	7 8 9
Koelreuteria paniculata, 5	7 8
Oxydendrum arboreum, 5	7 8
Rhododendron ferrugineum, 3	7 8
Teucrium chamaedrys, 5	7—10
* *Elsholtzia stauntonii*, 4	8 9 10
* *Sophora japonica*, 4	8
Hedera helix 'Arborescens', 5	9 10
* *Polygonum aubertii*, 4	9 10
Sarcococca ruscifolia, 7	11 12

13. Bird Attracting Plants

Although all dense growing plants will attract birds for nest building, those chosen here are the less troublesome species for landscape use. Those plants bearing fruit are so marked.

Acer campestre, zone 5	su-ss	any soil	good border
— *platanoides* 'Globosum', 5	su-ss	any soil	specimen
Alnus spp.	su-ss fr	humus	wet or dry
Amelanchier spp.	fr fl	any soil	specimen
Aronia spp.	fr	any soil	moist or shady
Berberis spp.	fr su	any soil	thorny hedges
Betula pendula, 2	su	humus	specimen
Carpinus betulus, 4		any soil	specimen or border
Clematis vitalba (and var.), 4	fl	any soil	needs support
Colutea arborescens, 5	su	any soil	dry areas
Cornus mas, 4	fr fl	any soil	dry areas
— *sanguinea*, 4	fr	humus	border plant
Cotoneaster spp.	fr	any soil	groundcover
Crataegus spp.	fr su	any soil	thorny border
Cytisus scoparius, 5	su	sandy	hillsides
Eleagnus spp.	su fr	any soil	good border
Euonymus spp.		any soil	hedge, groundcover
Gleditsia triacanthos, 4	su	sandy	shade tree
Hedera helix, 5	ss sh #	humus	vine, groundcover
Hippophae rhamnoides, 3	fr su	sandy	border
Ilex aquifolium, 5	fr #	humus	hedge, specimen
Ligustrum spp.	fr	any soil	hedge
Lonicera coerulea, 6	fr	any soil	hedge
— *xylosteum*, 4	fr sh	any soil	hedge
Lycium spp.	fr su ss	any soil	naturalizing
Malus spp.	fr fl su	any soil	border
Parthenocissus spp.	fr su	any soil	needs support
Photinia spp.	fr fl	humus	border
Pyrus communis, 4	fr su	any soil	border
Populus tremula, 2	su w	any soil	slopes
Prunus padus, 3	fr	any soil	border
— *spinosa*, 4	fr su	any soil	hedge
Quercus spp.	su	any soil	windbreak
Rhamnus catharticus, 4	fr su	any soil	border
— *frangula*, 2	fr	any soil	hedge
Rhus spp.	fr w	any soil	background
Ribes alpinum, 2	fr sh	any soil	hedges
Robinia spp.	su fl	any soil	slopes
Rosa spp.	fr fl	any soil	thorny hedge
Rubus fruticosus, 4	fr	humus	thorny hedge, slopes
Salix caprea, 4	su w	any soil	border, slopes
Sambucus nigra, 5	fr	any soil	border, slopes
— *racemosa*, 4	fr sh u	any soil	border
Sorbus aria, 5	fr su	any soil	gravel slopes

Forcing

— *aucuparia*, 2	fr su	any soil	specimen
— *torminalis*, 5	fr su	any soil	specimen
Spirea spp.	su	any soil	low border
Syringa vulgaris, 3	su fl	any soil	border
Viburnum opulus, 3	fr fl	any soil	border
— *trilobum*, 2	fr fl	any soil	border

CONIFERS

Juniperus spp.	fr # su	any soil	groundcover, border
Larix spp.	su	any soil	deciduous
Picea spp.	su #	any soil	windbreak
Taxus spp.	fr u #	any soil	hedge, low border
Thuja spp.	m #	any soil	hedge
Tsuga spp.	#	humus	border

14. Plants Suitable for Forcing Indoors

	best time	forcing period
Acer palmatum, zone 5	February—March	4—6 weeks
— *rubrum*, 3	after January	1—3 weeks
Aesculus hippocastanum, 3	after January	3—5 weeks
Amelanchier spp.	after December	3—5 weeks
Alnus rugosa, 2	after December	1—3 weeks
(Azalea) *Rhododendron indicum*, 6	after October	varying
— *japonicum*, 5	February—April	3—6 weeks
— 'Mollis' types	February—April	4—6 weeks
— 'Pontica' types	as above	as above
— 'Rustica' types	as above	as above
— 'Sinensis' types	as above	as above
Cercis canadensis, 4	after January	4—6 weeks
Chaenomeles spp.	after	1—3 weeks
Clematis (large flowering)	February—April	4—6 weeks
Cornus florida, 4	after December	4—6 weeks
— *mas*, 4	after December	2 weeks
Deutzia gracilis, 4	January—March	6 weeks
Enkianthus campanulatus, 4	February—April	4—7 weeks
Forsythia intermedia, 5	January—April	1—2 weeks
Hamamelis spp.	after December	1—3 weeks
Kalmia latifolia, 4	March—April	3—4 weeks
— *angustifolia*, 2	as above	as above
Laburnum 'Vossii', 5	February—April	6—8 weeks
Larix spp.	after January	6—8 weeks
Magnolia soulangiana, 5	December—March	1—3 weeks
— *stellata*, 5	after December	1—2 weeks
Malus spp.	February—March	4—5 weeks
Pieris japonica, 5	after December	2 weeks
Prunus glandulosa, 4	February—March	5—6 weeks

— *serrulata*, 5	January—March	1—3 weeks
— *triloba*, 5	December—March	3 weeks
Ribies alpinum, 2	after December	1—2 weeks
Rhododendron, (evergreen types)	January—March	4—8 weeks
Rosa (in pots)	February—April	8—10 weeks
Salix caprea, 4	after December	1—3 weeks
Syringa vulgaris, 3	October—May	3—6 weeks
Viburnum, most	December—March	5—6 weeks
Wisteria spp.	January—March	4—9 weeks

15. Plants for the Gravesite

Broadleaf Evergreens, see list p. 61
Specimen plants, see list p. 95.
Hedges, see list p. 114.
Groundcovers, see list p. 123.

Groundcovers (most important species)

Calluna vulgaris	zone 4	# fl su	see list p. 40
Cotoneaster dammeri	5	# fl su-ss of	
Dryas octopetala	4	# of fl su	
Erica carnea, types	4	# fl su-ss	
Euonymus fortunei 'Coloratus'	5	# of ss-sh	
— — 'Minimus'		# of ss-sh	
— — var. *radicans*		# of ss-sh	
Gaultheria procumbens	3	# of fl fr ss-sh	
Hypericum calycinum	6	# of fl ss-sh	
Hedera helix	5	# of ss-sh	
— — 'Sagittaefolia'		# of ss-sh	
Iberis sempervirens	5	# fl su	
Lonicera pileata	5	# of ss-sh	
Muehlenbeckia axillaris	7	# of	
Pachysandra terminalis	5	# of ss-sh	
Potentilla arbuscula	2	fl su	
Vinca minor	4	# of fl ss-sh	

Evergreen Conifers as Groundcover

Juniperus communis 'Repanda'	2	# su
— *horizontalis*	3	# su
— — 'Douglasii'		# su
— *procumbens* 'Nana'	5	# su
— *sabina* 'Tamariscifolia'	4	# su

Broadleaf Evergreens for Low Hedges

Berberis verruculosa	5	# of fl su-ss
— *buxifolia* 'Nana'	5	# of su
Lonicera nitida	7	# of su-ss

Sound Barriers

Lonicera nitida 'Graziosa'	zone 7	# of su-ss
Picea abies 'Nidiformis'	5	# of su (grows wide)
Pinus mugo pumilio	2	# of su (grows wide)
Teucrium chamaedrys	5	# of fl su

Taller Evergreens for the Outer Border

Ilex aquifolium, zone 5
— — 'Pyramidalis'
— *crenata*, 6
— *pernyi*, 6
Ligustrum ovalifolium, 5
— *vulgare* 'Atrovirens', 4
Lonicera nitida 'Elegant', 7
Chamaecyparis pisifera 'Plumosa', 3
— — 'Plumosa Aurea'
— — 'Squarrosa'
— — 'Boulevard'
Picea abies, 5
Long flowering season, see list p. 28
Fruiting plants, see list p. 74
Weeping habit, see list p. 13

Picea omorika, 4
— *pungens*, 2
Taxus baccata, 6
— — 'Fastigiata'
— *cuspidata capitata*, 4
— *media hicksii*, 4
Thuja occidentalis
— — 'Dark Green'
— — 'Techny'

16. Plants for Sound Barriers

Maximum noise buffering is achieved with the following plant qualities:

a) large leaves with strong branching character.

b) leaves curling on the edges or cupped.

c) dense branching and planting, perpendicular to sound source.

The choice of plants can also determine effective time of year.

a) species which hold their brown foliage all winter afford some winter protection. (i.e., Quercus, juvenile stage of Fagus, Carpinus)

b) coniferous evergreens provide a minimal effect year round. (Effect is better with very dense species.)

c) best for year round effect are broadleaf evergreens (i.e., *Viburnum rhytidophyllum* and *Rhododendron catawbiense*)

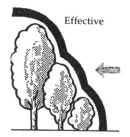

Effective

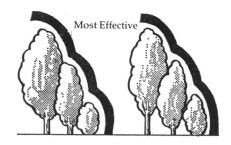

Most Effective

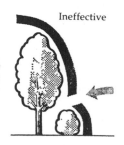

Ineffective

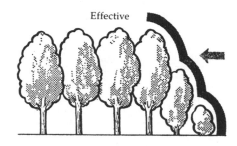

Effective

A noise barrier should be planted as near the sound source as possible, on a perpendicular line with a dense wall of foliage reaching to the ground. Alternate rows of foliage and dead air space provides best protection.

Plants for noise buffering capacity:

Acer platanoides
— psuedoplatanus
Alnus incana
Betula pendula
Carpinus betulus
Cornus alba
— sanguinea
Corylus avellana
Fagus silvatica
Juniperus pfitzeriana
Lonicera maackii
Philadelphus pubescens

Platanus acerifolia
Populus berolinensis
Pterocarya fraxinifolia
Quercus palustris
— robur
Rhododendron catawbiense
Ribies divaricatum
Sambucus nigra
Syringa vulgaris
Tilia platyphylla
Viburnum lantana
— rhytidophyllum

17. Plants for the Landscape

a. Trees

BROADLEAVES

Acer campestre (Hedge Maple)	zone 5, tolerates poor soil, low dense tree, good border
— *platanoides* (Norway Maple)	zone 3, deep rooted strong shade tree, good foliage
— *rubrum* (Red Maple)	zone 3, relatively fast growing, good fall color, shade tree, wet soil
— *saccharum* (Sugar Maple)	zone 3, good strong shade tree, needs good drainage, orange in fall
Aesculus hippocastanum (Horsechestnut)	zone 3, large shade tree, good for open areas, deep rooted, clay soil
Alnus glutinosa (Alder)	zone 3, deep moist humus or sandy soil, good foliage tree
— *incana*	zone 2, tolerates dryer more alkaline soil, otherwise as above
Betula papyrifera (Paper Birch)	zone 2, good white bark with age, more resistance to bronze birch borer
— *pendula* (European Birch)	zone 2, white on younger trees but very susceptible to birch borer in the Midwest.
— *maximowicziana* (Monarch Birch)	zone 5, good white, large catkins and leaves, resistant to borer
— *nigra* (River Birch)	zone 4, thin peeling cream colored bark, good borer resistance
Carpinus betulus (Hornbeam)	zone 4, strong shade tree, clean foliage, alkaline, moist soil
Crataegus spp. (Hawthorns)	very hardy small trees for flower, fruit, windbreak or wildlife planting; good on clay soil
Fagus silvatica (European Beech)	zone 4, better in cultivation than American Beech; large tree for humus soil, slow growing
Fraxinus excelsior (European Ash)	zone 3, strong wooded shade tree, moist or dry soil, alkaline, deep rooted
Fracinus pennsylvanica (Green Ash)	zone 2, good, strong, fast growing shade tree; use seedless varieties, any soil
— *americana* (White Ash)	zone 3, as above with purple fall foliage
Gleditsia triacanthos inermis (Thornless Honeylocust)	zone 4, fine leaved shade tree, rapid grower, pod and thorn free varieties available
Malus spp. (Crabapple)	zones 2—5, many varieties of excellent small flowering trees for specimen, windbreak and wildlife
Platanus acerifolia (London Planetree)	zone 5, very large, vigorous shade tree, any deep soil, one of the best fast growing shade trees

Populus alba
(White Poplar)
zone 3, very large, wide rapid growing tree, leaves white on underside

— *berolinensis*
(Berlin Poplar)
zone 2, good tree for difficult areas with temperature extremes, tall oval, deep rooted

— *tremula*
(Quaking Ash)
zone 2, best poplar for sandy soil, wet or dry, avoid mixing with pines

Prunus serrulata
(Oriental Cherry)
zone 5, many varieties available with single or double flowers, excellent specimen, humus soil

Prunus subhirtella
(Higan Cherry)
zone 5, many varieties available including autumn flowering and weeping forms, otherwise as above

Pyrus calleryana
(Callery Pear)
zone 4, excellent, hardy specimen flowering pears, good foliage and fall color, any soil

Quercus imbricaria
(Shingle Oak)
zone 5, strong, wide shade tree, glossy laural-like foliage, any soil

— *palustris*
(Pin Oak)
zone 4, low branched, fine texture tree, good screen or windbreak, avoid alkaline soil

— *robur*
(English Oak)
zone 5, deep rooted, strong shade tree, good foliage, slow grower

— *rubra* (Borealis)
(Red Oak)
zone 3, rapid growing oak, large tree, red fall foliage

Salix alba
(White Willow)
zone 2, varieties as Weeping Willow picturesque in wide open space, will help dry up wet areas, not for small lawns

Sorbus aucuparia
(European Mt. Ash)
zone 2, excellent specimen, good flower, fruit and foliage, humus soil, good drainage

Tilia cordata
(Littleleaf Linden)
zone 3, good strong shade tree, rounded, fragrant in flower

Tilia platyphyllos
(Bigleaf Linden)
zone 3, faster growing, large leaves otherwise as above

Ulmus carpinifolia
(Smooth-leaved Elm)
zone 4, many varieites available some resistant to Dutch Elm disease, some slender uprights for street use

— *parvifolia*
(Chinese Elm)
zone 5, excellent shade tree, resistant to Dutch Elm Disease, much underrated and confused with the weak wooded Siberian Elm

CONIFERS

Abies concolor
(White Fir)
zone 4, more heat tolerant than most firs, excellent ornamental, soft bluishcolor

Larix decidua
(European Larch)
zone 2, deciduous conifer, deep rooted in any soil, interesting ornamental

Picea abies
(Norway Spruce)
zone 4, good dark green color, dense, rapid growing young tree being more open with age

Shrubs for the Landscape

— *pungens*
(Colorado Spruce)

zone 2, denser, slower growing tree with gray-green to blue color

Pinus cembra
(Swiss Stone Pine)

zone 2, very slow growing, a dense dark green pyramid, excellent ornamental

Pinus nigra
(Austrian Pine)

zone 4, fast growing, excellent windbreak or specimen tree on any soil, best transplanted when young

— *sylvestris*
(Scotch Pine)

zone 2, irregular growing if not sheared, open at maturity with attractive reddish bark, any soil

— *strobus*
(White Pine)

zone 3, soft green foliage, easy to transplant, fast growing, good windbreak, takes shearing well

b. Shrubs
(* denotes small trees)

BROADLEAVES

*Amelanchier laevis**
(Serviceberry)

zone 4, excellent small specimen tree for flower, fruit and fall foliage, oval upright, any soil

Berberis thunbergii
(Japanese Barberry)

zone 4, very serviceable plant with many varieties, any soil, dry conditions, good hedge

*Cornus mas**
(Cornelian Cherry Dogwood)

zone 4, very early flowering small specimen, any soil, very hardy

— *sanguinea*
(Bloodtwig Dogwod)

zone 4, shade tolerant, any soil, wet or dry, good fall color, tall shrub

Corylus avellana
(Hazelnut)

zone 3, 'Contorta' variety is interesting specimen, otherwise good for sun or shade, any soil

Cotoneaster apiculata
(Cranberry Coton.)

zone 4, good hardy species for 2' groundcover, sun or shade, red fruit in fall, any soil

— *dammeri*

zone 5, evergreen species of many-varieties, small flowers, low, prefers semi-shade, out of wind

*Crataegus phaenopyrum**
(Washington Hawthorn)

zone 4, very sturdy, vigorous plant for specimen or screen, flower fruit and fall color, thorny

Cytisus scoparius
(Scotch Broom)

zone 5, best in full sun, good drainage, yellow flowers and green stems, tolerates dry mineral soil

Euonymus alatus
(Burning Bush)

zone 3, good hedge or specimen in full sun, heavy soil, nice branching structure, good red fall color

Forsythia intermedia
(Forsythia)

zone 5, vigorous hedging plant with profuse yellow flowers in spring, varieties and dwarf species available

Hippophae rhamnoides
(Sea Buckthorn)

zone 3, grows on the poorest sandy mineral soil, dry, sunny, good foliage and fruit effect

Hydrangea macrophylla

zone 5, low bushy plant, glossy foliage, humus soil, large flowers pink or blue depending on soil acidity (blue in acid soil)

Ilex aquifolium*
(English Holly)

zone 6, many varieties available, dislikes hot dry conditions, grown for glossy evergreen foliage and red berries, cross pollination needed for fruit

Ilex opaca*
(American Holly)

zone 5, as above, slightly hardier, prefers sandy humus, also having many varieties

Ligustrum vulgare
(Common Privet)

zone 4, very serviceable plant, good hedge, easily grown on any soil

Lonicera alpigena
(Dwarf Alps Honeysuckle)

zone 5, moist but well drained soil, full sun, good for large rock garden

— *maackii*
(Amur Honeysuckle)

zone 2, good screening plant, holding leaves late, glossy foliage, vigorous on any soil

— *tatarica*
(Tatarian Honeysuckle)

zone 3, more common but highly rated screen plant, vigorous on any soil, varieties available

— *xylosteum* 'Claveyi'
(Clavey's Dwarf H.)

zone 4, low dense hedging plant, easy to grow

Magnolia soulangeana*
(Saucer Magnolia)

zone 5, very popular plant for its large pink flowers, rounded habit, good specimen on humus soil, varieties available

— *stellata*
(Star Magnolia)

zone 5, very hardy species, dense bushy plant, excellent white flowers, good on heavy mineral soil

Philadelphus spp.
(Mockorange)

zones 3—5, good screen plants including some dwarf types, flowers fragrant, takes dry mineral soil

Potentilla fruticosa
(Bush Cinquefoil)

zone 2, excellent small shrub for full sun, yellow flowers all summer, good on heavy clay soil, red and white varieties available

Prunus × cistena
(Purple Sand Cherry)

zone 2, popular purple foliage plant, very hardy, vigorous on any soil

— *glandulosa*
(Flowering Almond)

zone 4, masses of pink flowers in early spring, full sun, good on heavy soil

— *laurocerasus*
(Laurel-cherry)

zone 6, glossy evergreen hedging plant, needs humus soil out of wind and winter sun

Pyracantha coccinea
(Firethorn)

zone 6, thorny shrub grown for bright red berries in fall, excellent espalier on a sunny wall, semi-evergreen prefers protection

Rhododendron spp.

zones 2—7, very attractive plants in foliage and flower, hardy but must have

Shrubs for the Landscape

Rosa chinensis 'Minima'
(Fairy Rose)

— *rugosa*
(Rogusa Rose)

Salix caprea
(Goat Willow)

Spirea spp.

Syringa spp.
(Lilacs)

Viburnum × burkwoodii
(Burkwood Viburnum)

— *carlesi*
(Koreanspice Viburnum)

— *opulus*
(European Cranberrybush)

Viburnum prunifolium
(Blackhaw Vib.)

— *tinus*
(Laurustinus)

— *triloba*
(American Cranberrybush)

good drainage, acid soil and protection from winter winds and sun, many species and varieties

zone 5, pink summer flowering species, good low fronting plant, fine texture, full sun, heavy soil

zone 2, very hardy attractive border plant, flowers all summer, fruits in fall, good foliage

zone 4, large yellow catkins in spring, vigorous grower on moist or heavy soil

zones 4—7, pink or white summer flowering shrubs from 30cm to 3m, need full sun, good on clay soil

zones 2—5, many species and varieties of fragrant spring flowering shrubs; good border plants, vigorous on heavy alkaline soils

zone 5, semi-evergreen with very fragrant flowers in May, glossy foliage, any soil

zone 4, fragrant flowers, larger dull green deciduous leaves, dense plant to 2m

zone 3, large white flowering border plant, fruit for wildlife, red fall foliage, dwarf forms available

zone 3, large open shrub, attractive foliage, flowers, fruit and fall foliage, good specimen

zone 7, more tender but excellent plant for flower, fruit and glossy foliage, evergreen

zone 2, similar to European Cranberrybush, but hardier with edible fruits, dwarf types avail.

CONIFERS

Juniperus chinensis
(Chinese Juniper)

— *communis*
(Common Juniper)

— *horizontalis*
(Creeping Juniper)

— *sabina*
(Savin Juniper)

Pinus mugo
(Mugo Pine)

zone 4, many types from low groundcovers to large wide shrubs, very serviceable plants in full sun and heavy dry soil

zone 2, species with some low but mostly upright forms, otherwise as above

zone 2, many vigorous groundcover types, bluish foliage, otherwise as above

zone 4, low wide types with bright moss green foliage, else as above

zone 2, very attractive and hardy coniferous shrubs, growing wide and large with age unless true dwarf variety, full sun, any well drained soil

Taxus × *media*
   (Anglojap Yew)

— *cuspidata*
   (Japanese Yew)

zone 4, many varieties of dense dark green evergreens, good hedge or background plant, shade or sun, any well drained soil

zone 4, as above but generally more upright, many varieties available